P9-DYZ-587

WILLIAMSBURG

My Town

WILLIAMSBURG

MY TOWN

Fred L. Frechette

Fred L. Frechette

ISBN-13: 978-0-9790369-0-3
ISBN-10: 0-9790369-0-9

Printed in Canada

The Dietz Press, Richmond, Virginia

Photographs not otherwise credited are the author's.
Book design by Susan Bracey Sheppard, WordsRight
and Bob Sheppard, Communication Graphics
Map by Donald Ferguson

In memory

Vernon Meredith Geddy

1897–1952

and his daughter

Caroline Cole Geddy Frechette

1929–1994

Table of Contents

FOREWARD

It was my long-time friend, talented writer Will Molineux, who urged me to put my typing fingers where my mouth is and record some of the anecdotes with which I'd been deafening him over the years. Thus he was this book's genesis. Then, to protect himself, he became my backup editor and fact-checker. I could no more have written this book and assembled its illustrations without his help than I could have operated the Williamsburg Bureau of the *Richmond Times-Dispatch* without him in his undergraduate days at William and Mary.

Writing a book without an editor is like driving an automobile without brakes. Thus Monica Hagan of El Cajon, CA, kept me safely in the road. Her advice and corrections were invaluable.

When I employ the terms 'Colonial Williamsburg', 'the Restoration', or 'CW', I refer to the organization originally funded by John D. Rockefeller, Jr., which restored and reconstructed buildings in the historic parts of Williamsburg. It is now officially Colonial Williamsburg Foundation.

Virginia is the only state in the union in which incorporated cities are not part of any county and vice versa. Thus when this book refers to Williamsburg, it generally means greater Williamsburg, which includes adjacent parts of James City and York Counties. In this respect, I mimic the U.S. Post Office, which uses Williamsburg as the mailing address for residents of these neighboring areas.

If this book occasionally strays into subjects outside the immediate area of Williamsburg, it's because I recall them as bits of knowledge that helped me understand what Virginia is all about.

It goes without saying but bears stating that the contents of this book reflect only my own opinions and attitudes. It also goes without saying that I did not at the time record the quotations I've put into the mouths of people about whom I've written, but I did my best to reconstruct their statements accurately.

F.L.F.

Vernon Meredith Geddy
1897–1952

Chapter One

The Wonderful World of Vernon Geddy

In the spring of 1945, during my junior year at William and Mary in Williamsburg, Virginia, I went to get a haircut in Barnes Barber Shop, which was on the second floor above Albert Douglas's bakery on Duke of Gloucester Street. Charlie and the other barbers were busy, so I sat in one of the chairs against the wall to wait my turn.

I hadn't been there more than a few minutes when a middle-aged man about my size, wearing a neat business suit, entered the shop and sat beside me. With no delay, he greeted me with a friendly grin, stuck out his hand and said, in his wonderful Tidewater drawl, "I'm Vernon Geddy."

Like anyone old enough to be in college, I knew the Geddy name, for he was executive vice president of Colonial Williamsburg, the man in charge when President Kenneth Chorley was in New York, which was more than half of every year. He was also senior warden of the vestry of Bruton Parish Church, a member of the board of directors of Williamsburg's only bank, former city councilman and commonwealth's attorney (known in other states as district attorney). Thus he was probably the best-known and most influential man in town — and here he was, prepared to wait for his turn in a barber chair and offering to shake hands with an unknown college student. His marvelous warmth overcame my awe and I managed to shake his hand and identify myself.

"You write a column in *The Flat Hat*," he said, referring to the William and Mary undergraduate weekly newspaper.

"Yessir."

"I really liked what you wrote about the Travis House," he said, which blew my mind. Not only had he read the college weekly, he noticed and remembered my column. Our conversation went on from there, and my love and esteem for this man blossomed. Vernon Geddy epitomized for me, then and now, all that was good, noble and honorable in a Southern gentleman. Geddy had a deep sense of honor, resigning from the city council when he joined the CW staff to avoid any conflict of interest. No one I know ever came close to matching his genial charm, good humor and respect for others — and I never met anyone who knew the man and didn't like him.

My hometown, by choice, is Williamsburg. It's probably as familiar to Americans as any other town in America. Restored to its 1776 appearance — a time when it ranked with Boston, Philadelphia and New York — it has become a national shrine and attracted millions of visitors. Note that I *chose* Williamsburg. That's because I had no home town of my own. By the time I arrived in the 'Burg at the age of twenty I had lived in twelve different towns, none of which was a community I could call mine.

A hometown is as much a state of mind as it is a dictionary definition. It's Mark Twain's Hannibal, Missouri; Dwight Eisenhower's Abilene, Kansas; *The Music Man*'s River City, Iowa; or any of a thousand similar places, real, imagined or adopted. It's a self-contained community, a place where you might not be on a first-name basis with all who live there, but you know who they are and they know you. It's a community that meets most basic needs — doctors, dentists, police, etc. — and local businesses provide residents with adequate goods and services.

My experience in Williamsburg goes back to the time when its area population was about 6,000 — including patients at a state mental hospital located within the city. The town contained William and Mary, which enrolled 1,200 students, but they weren't counted. Medical services were provided by a tiny private hospital and about four doctors. We also boasted three or four lawyers and were protected by six policemen and an all-volunteer fire department.

As of this writing that 6,000 population of 1942 has grown, according to estimates, to more than 60,000. We now have 62 hotels and motels, 31 bed & breakfast establishments, 5 guest homes, 4 campgrounds and 15 golf courses. Two large hospitals are under construction and the yellow pages of the telephone directory list doctors and lawyers too numerous to count.

Vernon Geddy's life, though tragically short — 1897 to 1952 — encompassed a critical period in Williamsburg's history. He played a very important role in most of the formative years of the Restoration and, before that, was a participant and keen observer of life in the pre-Rockefeller years. He grew up playing on the streets of Williamsburg, attended William and Mary, and was a lifelong friend of another key player in the town's history, Henry Morris 'Polly' Stryker, Williamsburg's mayor for twenty years.

Geddy had an incredible memory. I don't think he ever forgot anyone he ever met, anything he ever heard or any word he ever read. I learned this early in my association with him. He and his wife often took pity on me and fed me at their Holly Hill home on Jamestown Road

Colonial Williamsburg Foundation

During World War II, Vernon Geddy escorts Mrs. Winston Churchill.

when their daughter Caroline was away at college. I had no automobile, but Geddy would pick me up in either his black Buick or the 'Yellow Peril', his older wooden Ford station wagon.

The first time I was ever their guest, after we finished dessert, I began to help clear the dining room table. Geddy grabbed me by the arm and dragged me into the tiny sitting room which was his favorite hangout. I protested that I wanted to help with the dishes and he shook his head, whispering, "If you don't know how, they can't ask you."

For many reasons, not the least because of his entertaining manner, he was in demand as a speechmaker. Usually his subject had to do with Williamsburg's restoration. For this, he had an all-purpose speech, which he called 'Old 37', because that was the year in which it was written. He easily adapted it to every kind of audience, from garden to Rotary clubs, by changing a few lines.

One evening he had to leave Holly Hill soon after dinner to deliver a talk for which Old 37 was not appropriate. His public relations director, Bela Norton, wrote a new speech for the occasion. It covered about a dozen or more pages, which were neatly bound together. After dinner, while his wife prepared herself for the public appearance, I sat with him in the sitting room. He had Norton's speech in his lap. I figured he would study it to familiarize himself with it, but all he did was riffle through the pages once. A few minutes later, when we got up to leave, he left the speech on the seat of his chair.

I indicated the bound pages. "You're forgetting your speech."

He laughed. "Never."

A day or two later, I asked Bob Hoke, who had been in the audience, how the speech went. Bob, one of Bela Norton's staff, had probably had a hand in writing it. He said Geddy was letter-perfect. He had apparently memorized the speech in the few moments it took for him to riffle through its pages.

Geddy invariably described the Duke of Gloucester Street he knew as a boy as "99 feet wide and two feet deep." And he was a fountain of colloquialisms he picked up mainly from the country folk he worked with as commonwealth's attorney. I've been kicking myself ever since his death for not recording more of them, like his admonition, applicable in many situations, "If you got an itch, scratch it."

When he nosed around the kitchen to see how things were coming along for dinner, he might ask for a 'smidgin' of something he relished. He explained to me that a smidgin was more than a pinch but less than a spoonful. One of his favorite dishes was 'simlins', a preparation of squash and onions, fried, I think, in bacon grease. Confronted with a large portion of food, he was apt to comment, "Us eat all that, us bust!" And if he offered you one of his special foods and you refused it, he'd grin and tell you, "Fine, there's too many what like it already." Another favorite was hot cakes, almost always accompanied by, "hot cakes make the butter fly."

If one showed too much anticipation for a trip — even a drive to Richmond — he described it as being 'journey proud'. That, he told me, was a term used to describe going to the depot to wait for a train not due to leave for at least two hours. One of his favorites was an admonition he gave to people who had received praise or recognition for an outstanding accomplishment: "Let it go to your heart, not your head." He lived that.

Geddy's law school education, experience as commonwealth's attorney and exposure to the Yankees who accompanied Mr. Rockefeller's millions to Williamsburg took the sharp edges off his drawl. Thus he had a modified Tidewater accent which seemed a perfect fit for his personality.

Early in our life together, my wife did her best to educate me about Tidewater customs, habits and manners. From the beginning she let me know that there was no such thing as a single, all-purpose Southern drawl. Caroline said real Southerners rolled in the aisles with laughter when a movie actress attempted to speak in a drawl. She told me there were more different kinds of drawl than I could count and that people with good ears could tell what part of the South a person came from just by listening to his or her speech.

Caroline, like her father, had Americanized her Virginia Tidewater drawl but she could still speak it. As she told me, "If I want to use a Tidewater drawl to tell you I came down the stairs combing my hair," she said, "it would sound like 'Ah came down the sty-uhs coamin' mah hy-uh'."

That should have prepared me for Auntie — that's what Caroline called her great aunt — but it didn't. Like many older residents in the first half of the 20th century, she had speech habits acquired in the years after the Civil War. Caroline Lane Cole, who lived her entire life in Williamsburg, was born in the late 1860s and survived into the 1950s as a perfect specimen of a Southern lady, speaking an unabridged Virginia Tidewater drawl.

If Auntie ever lifted a hand other than to direct her servants, I never saw it. Her every meal was prepared and served by a live-in cook. Not that Mrs. Cole was arrogant, ugly or demanding. She was a consummate lady, always polite, always gentle, whether speaking to a servant or to the mayor.

Caroline interpreted and explained some of her mannerisms. One of the idiosyncrasies of an authentic Virginia Tidewater drawl was the speaker's habit of inserting a 'y' sound in certain words. For instance, when Auntie spoke, 'Garden Club' became 'Gyawden Club'. Another confusing usage was Auntie's reference to taking a railroad trip as 'takin' the cyaws' — taking the cars.

Mrs. Cole's late husband, Henry Denison Cole, who had a store across Duke of Gloucester Street from Bruton Parish Church, was a town councilman and pillar of the church. He provided streetside benches for the Pulaski Club between his shop and home. In the early part of the 1900s, the Pulaski Club consisted of some of Williamsburg's leading citizens. Membership in this influential group was by invitation only.

Cole's father had acquired considerable property south of the town. Although the portion on the Williamsburg side of College Creek was given to his younger brother, Cole retained a large piece on the opposite side. Upon his death, Mrs. Cole inherited it. About 1950, she sold sixty acres to the Sisters of Mercy, who established Walsingham Academy upon the site. When Route 199 cut off part of the property, Williamsburg Landing acquired the loose parcel. About half the rest became the Holly Hills subdivision; the remaining half — a beautiful wooded area along College Creek — was purchased by the city for ultimate use as a park and nature preserve.

Although he was known by everyone else as 'Den' Cole, Auntie always referred to her late husband as 'Mr. Cole'. And when she became an avid fan of William and Mary football in the 1940s, Auntie never missed radio broadcasts of its games and often spoke of its leading athletes — referring to them as 'Mistoo Korzowski, Mistoo Magdziak, Mistoo Piefke, Mistoo Mackewicz' and the like. She was truly a living artifact of the Victorian era in Williamsburg.

Although the town Vernon Geddy knew as a youth had progressed a bit beyond what it was like when Auntie was a teen, it was still quite rural. As he put it to me, "Williamsburg was a lovely little college town with only about a thousand inhabitants — about 150 to 200 students at the college and about 600 inmates at the hospital. No one had any money to speak of, but everyone seemed to live comfortably and happily. It was such a quiet, peaceful place that time stood still. In fact, the town actually forgot to hold an election in 1912."

Rather sheepishly, he added, "My father was involved in the oversight, for he was clerk of the court. But about three in the afternoon he remembered it was election day, and somehow or other managed to scurry around and get the new town council elected.

"Newspapers learned about it, of course, and chided Williamsburg, which they called 'Lotusburg'. I like to think that they envied us."

In his teens, Geddy attended William and Mary. "Pride in its past didn't go very far toward paying its operating costs or paving the way toward a promising future," he said. "In fact, some folks didn't think the college had any future at all."

His friend Polly Stryker was also a student. Both played on the football team, such as it was. Together they told me about their historic game against the University of Delaware in 1915, which William and Mary lost by the score of 73 to 0, probably the worst beating any W&M football team ever suffered. They laughed about it because, although they were humiliated at the time, they agreed there was some consolation in having participated in a game that would go down in history.

Geddy went on to the University of Virginia Law School. Stryker enrolled at the Medical College of Virginia School of Dentistry. In the early 1920s they were together again, with second-floor offices in the Peninsula Bank building on Duke of Gloucester Street near the 1700s courthouse which in those days was in everyday use.

In pre-restoration days, the area around the old courthouse and Powder Magazine was the center of Williamsburg's business district. The town's hotel stood where Chowning's Tavern now stands. A mixture — there was no zoning — of garages, offices, stores and churches were scattered haphazardly around the area.

Although Geddy never told a lie, I suspect he enjoyed improving on facts in order to tell a better story. Thus, when he wanted to impress his listener with the rustic nature of Williamsburg when he began practicing law, his narrative went like this: "Things were so slow that Polly and I would often get together in my office for a game or two of checkers. If we heard someone climbing the stairs toward our offices, Polly would say, 'Sh-sh-sh, if he doesn't hear us, he might go away.'

"There wasn't much money in Williamsburg. If I made a dollar on Monday and put it in the bank, it probably passed through the hands of most people in town, then I'd get it back in my hands the following Monday."

Of course things weren't quite as rustic as Geddy described, but when he was appointed commonwealth's attorney, court cases were so few and far between it was only a part-time job. Later, he said, it became busier when the government began prosecuting moonshiners. Although only in his twenties, his winning personality and intelligence, combined with other fine qualities, earned him a leading role in the community. Most important, he won the trust of the rector of Bruton Parish Church — and a leading role in the conversion of Williamsburg from a sleepy, forgotten village to an internationally known tourist attraction.

Vernon Geddy told me a whole lot about the Williamsburg he knew as a boy and young man. He rarely made reference to things of which he had no firsthand knowledge, so his recollections were pure gold, like the things he remembered about the Reverend Dr. W.A.R. Goodwin and John D. Rockefeller, Jr. He kept it all in perspective however, because he knew Williamsburg's background.

Before Jamestown — America's Forgotten Indians

This book is not intended to be a schoolbook history, but to understand and appreciate the Williamsburg of today, it is helpful to reach back and take a look at its roots — roots that are only six miles away, on Jamestown Island. In 1607 that's where the English established their first permanent settlement in America.

Almost everyone knows at least a smattering about Jamestown (not counting those who show up asking to see Plymouth Rock). Most folks have probably heard of Pocahontas, but not many know much more about the Indians who were living in the area when the English

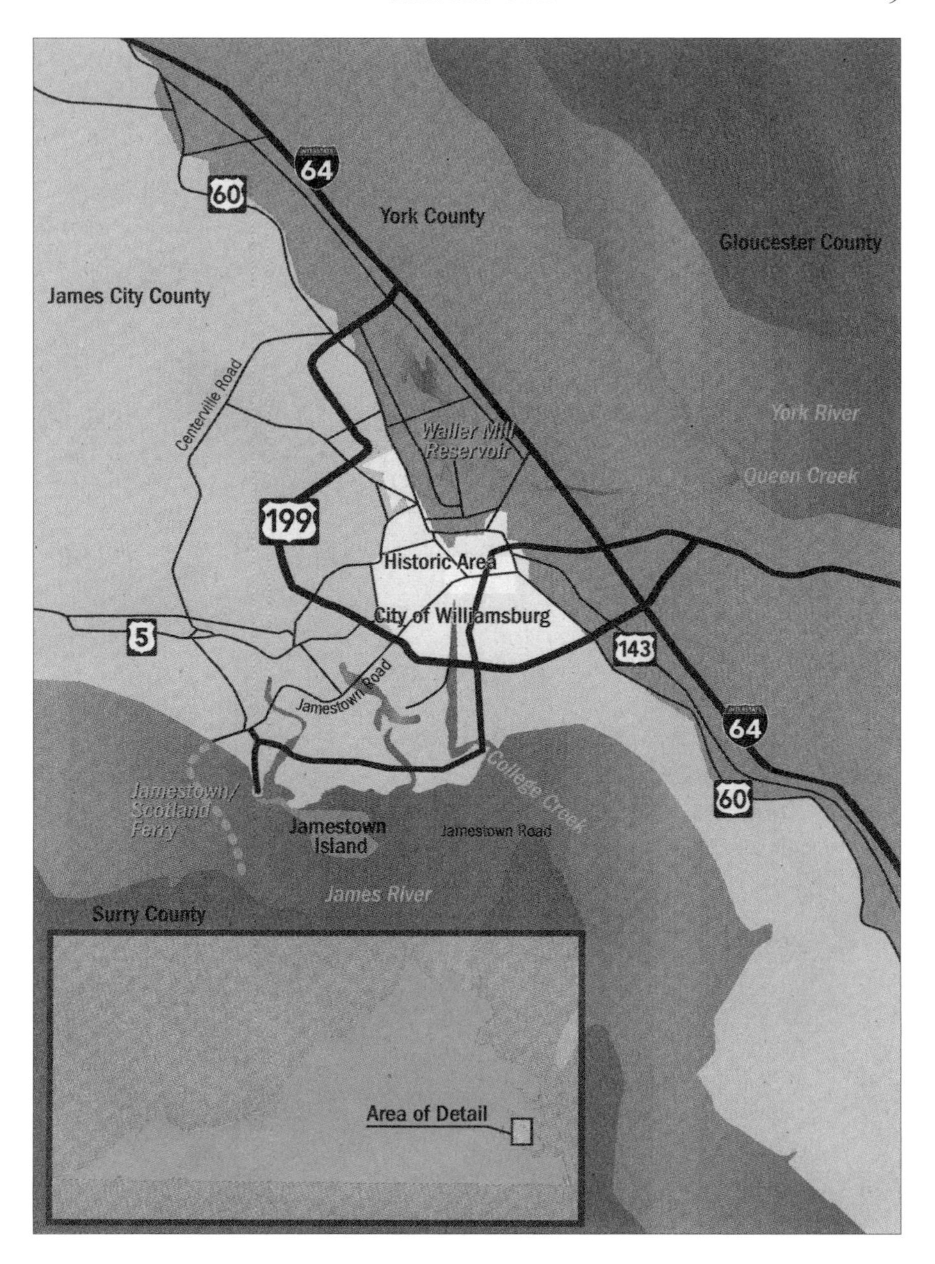

Map of Williamsburg area.

arrived. They are probably unaware that these alleged savages developed two incredibly important crops. One was corn. The other was tobacco which, although discredited today, was vital to the economic growth of Virginia and neighboring colonies.

One of the most knowledgeable experts on the subject of Tidewater Indians I ever met was Dr. Ben C. McCary, a professor of modern languages at William and Mary. We became friends when I helped him with some photography. In the process he shared with me some of his encyclopedic knowledge.

The Indians living around Jamestown were members of the Powhatan Confederacy. Powhatan, a remarkably able and crafty ruler, started out with a handful of tribes near the present site of Richmond. By 1607 he had conquered and united more than thirty Algonquian tribes with an estimated population of 9,000. His confederation controlled a huge area of coastal Virginia and North Carolina. From the Potomac River on the north to Currituck Sound on the south, between the fall line and the ocean, Powhatan's people flourished in more than 200 villages. They developed a thriving agricultural economy and well-defined culture.

This was the country invaded by the English. Powhatan did not go to war and drive them out because Captain John Smith persuaded him that the Jamestown settlement was only temporary. (If Powhatan had chosen otherwise, Jamestown might have become another Lost Colony. Just 21 years earlier, an English settlement on Roanoke Island in North Carolina — close to Powhatan's Confederacy — vanished completely.)

Not only did the Indians permit the English to stay, they helped keep them alive by providing food during the critical early months of the settlement. As the years passed, Powhatan awoke to the fact that the Europeans had no intention of giving up their foothold in Virginia, but the marriage of his daughter Pocahontas to John Rolfe halted any ideas he might have had of driving away the settlers.

Pocahontas' death in 1617, followed by Powhatan's a year later, ended the years of peace. But in the ten years since their arrival, the strength of the English had increased tremendously while the Indians had weakened, mainly because European diseases like smallpox had decimated them. In spite of this, they tried twice — in 1622 and 1644 — to massacre or drive out the colonists. It turned out to be a massacre — but of the Indians. A few survivors of Powhatan's Confederacy were driven into the swamps, their villages and crops obliterated.

Though they were never again a factor in the history of Virginia, these forgotten Indians left indelible marks. Lilting, musical names used to identify geographic features remain: Accomac, Chesapeake,

Chincoteague, Kecoughtan, Kiptopeke and Pungoteague. Motorists driving in eastern Virginia cross rivers named Chickahominy, Mattaponi, Nansemond, Pamunkey, Piankatank, Potomac and Rappahannock.

I had no idea of the pervasiveness of those pre-Jamestown Indians until my wife Caroline kicked up some strange-looking stone chips years ago as we walked along the shore of the James River. A few days later she showed them to an archaeologist at Jamestown. He identified them as discarded efforts by some frustrated Indian to fashion a spear or arrowhead.

Without belittling Caroline's stone chips, he explained it was not at all unusual to find such chips in Tidewater. He said the Indians had scores of small settlements where they remained until they used up the soil nutrients they needed to grow their corn and tobacco. Then they'd simply move their settlement to a more fertile location. Over the centuries, such habits ensured that Indians sooner or later occupied all the arable land in Tidewater, not just once, but repeatedly.

Stanley Hula, a Charles City County farmer, told me that in the days before no-till agriculture, local farmers constantly plowed up stone chips. This is not only proof that the Indians lived everywhere around Williamsburg at one time or another, it is also proof that shaping arrowheads or spear tips from rocks must have been one of the most maddening jobs in the world.

Most Tidewater land seems to consist mainly of sand, gravel or clay, so I asked historian Douglass Adair where Powhatan's Indians found the rocks they used to make their weapons and tools. His answer: Indians living above the fall line of the rivers, where stones were plentiful, probably loaded rafts with rocks and floated down to Tidewater to trade for corn, tobacco and shellfish.

Caroline and I found confirmation of this. While beach-walking along the James on a February afternoon during a neap tide — meaning the water was very low — we stumbled over a scattering of boulders protruding from the muddy bottom. They were large. I could barely lift one. Since they were not indigenous, we realized they must have been delivered — probably shoved off their raft — by up-country Indians. We surmised that the local Indians, recipients of the shipment, were too smart to carry all those heavy stones twenty feet up the bluff to their village. They knew the pile wouldn't move, so they simply removed them from the river as needed, one at a time.

The Indian rebellions, though crushed with tragic consequences for the natives, did not kill them all. Dr. McCary took me to visit surviving tribal groups. Descendents of Powhatan's Confederacy received such shabby treatment over the years it's a miracle any of them preserved their tribal identities. To do so, they had to overcome a huge handicap: They did not look like the popular notion of Northern or Western Indians. Powhatan's Indians, according to descriptions written by the early settlers, were "dusky", not red, with straight black hair.

Their appearance, so much like that of Africans, impelled some officials in the Commonwealth of Virginia to declare in the 1920s that there were no real Indians in the state, only Negroes pretending to be Indians. This official position made it next to impossible for the surviving descendents of Powhatan's Confederacy to educate their children in public schools.

In those days before integration, every city and county in Virginia had to provide two separate school systems, one white, one black. Even before I made my first visit to Charles City County as a reporter back in 1952, I had been told that it was probably the poorest of Virginia's one hundred counties. For this reason I was dumbfounded to learn that Charles City, which could barely support the required two school systems, had three: white, black and Indian.

This came about because the Indians flatly refused to send their children to the black schools and, since they were officially consider black, they could not be admitted to the white school (there was only one). The county couldn't afford to support an entire system for them, but the Indians, mainly Chickahominies, raised enough money to build Samaria School, which offered grades one through eight. I can't recall how the teachers were paid, but I did find out that for Indian boys and girls who wanted to go to high school, the county provided one-way railroad coach tickets to an institution on an Oklahoma reservation.

When he learned of the situation, Russell M. Carneal of Williamsburg, who represented Charles City (as well as Williamsburg and James City County) in the Virginia General Assembly, was able to change things. In 1954, Virginia officially recognized that some of its citizens were indeed Indians and set up specifications by which they could be identified. Virginia Indians must prove to the Bureau of Vital Statistics that their veins and arteries carry a required percentage of

Newport News Daily Press

After representing Williamsburg in the Virginia General Assembly, Russ Carneal (right) *became a circuit court judge here. Accompanying him is Bill Person, who served as commonwealth's attorney, then also became a circuit court judge.*

authentic Indian blood. Otherwise, they're not officially Indians. (Not everyone agrees with this, but perhaps some day DNA testing will sort it out.)

In Charles City County, Chief Oliver O. Adkins of the Chickahominy Tribe showed me a handwritten ledger dating back to the mid 1800s which was a roster of the members of his tribe. He indicated some names that had been crossed out because the man or woman in question had married a black and was permanently expelled from the tribe. In King William County, Chief Tecumseh Lightfoot Cook of the Pamunkeys, who himself looked very much like a weatherbeaten white farmer, presided over reservation residents who seemed quite light-skinned. I wasn't as familiar with Chief Custalow's people at the nearby Mattaponi Reservation, but had no trouble accepting all of them as Indians.

In spite of the daunting adversity they faced over the years, Virginia's Tidewater Indians earned admiration in many quarters. I remember asking Sheriff Lampkin of Charles City what kind of experience he'd had with Indians. I've never forgotten his reply: "None." In other words, they never gave him any trouble. Another time I met a successful Richmond manufacturer of restaurant furniture. He told me that his factory employed only Indians, most of them Chickahominies from Charles City, because "they're honest, they're reliable and they're conscientious."

This sort of character is exemplified each November when the Pamunkey and Mattaponi chiefs deliver to Virginia's governor a token tribute for the use of their reservations. The gifts, which take the form of game, fish or fur, date to colonial era treaties. The Commonwealth of Virginia ignored those treaties for years — but not the Indians. They never forgot their promises, but sadly, they'd lost much of their heritage, for when they went up the steps of the state capitol in Richmond, for many years they were clad in the regalia of Western Plains Indians.

Researchers have resurrected authentic pictures of what Powhatan's Indians really wore when the English arrived at Jamestown. Unfortunately, those fashions may never become popular. The women went topless.

Jamestown-Yorktown Foundation

Semi-authentic attire as worn by historical interpreters at Jamestown Settlement in the re-creation of an Indian home of Chief Powhatan's era.

Middle Plantation – Not Forgotten, Just Ignored

With suppression of the Indians, Jamestown's status as capital of the Virginia colony was secured politically and militarily — but not from fever and fire. Its nearby swamps assured a plentiful supply of fever-bearing mosquitoes. As if that weren't enough, residents of Jamestown who survived malaria and other death-dealing diseases were fire prone. Historians haven't figured out why, but the record is clear: Conflagrations were as frequent as fevers. Without effective prevention and means to extinguish them, fires made all Jamestown's buildings potential — often actual — ash heaps almost as soon as erected.

During the 1600s some settlers found healthier, safer homes on nearby high ground between the James and York Rivers, an area which became known as Middle Plantation and before long supported at least one tavern and a church, Bruton Parish. Thus Middle Plantation acquired an identity of its own, but I never heard much about it during my early years in this area. It was as if the Williamsburg of 1776 magically materialized out of the wilderness.

I used to enjoy watching Jim Knight at work. Employed by Colonial Williamsburg, this native of Yorktown was a draftsman by profession who became an archaeologist by necessity. The Restoration put him in charge of mapping all the sites in the historic area, so he was almost always busy supervising a small crew — usually six men — excavating old foundations. He covered the town foot by foot — a foot wide and a foot deep — during his CW career. That was the size of the trenches his men dug seeking old foundations. The dimensions were dictated by the width of shovels and the average depth down to undisturbed hardpan, the concrete-like clay which underlays local land.

Jim used the Frenchman's Map — drawn by French Army engineers after the Battle of Yorktown — and other research to get an idea of what to seek, then he put his crew to work digging trenches diagonally across the property in question. Whatever he uncovered, he recorded on a plat with his rule and transit.

"The foundations almost never true up," he said. "Those old boys built everything by eye. One side of a building almost always measures a few inches longer or shorter than the other."

I recall an occasion when the foundations his men were exposing seemed completely out of sync, crossing each other in a confusing manner. I joked with Jim, saying something on the order of, "I guess that guy's wife couldn't make up her mind where to build the new room."

Jim laughed. "You're way off on that guess." He pointed to one of the foundations. "This here was built nearly a hundred years before that one." He indicated the other row of bricks. He explained that the first dated to the 1600s, the second to the 1700s. He added that there were many such traces of 1600s buildings in and around Williamsburg.

It never occurred to me to ask Jim if he recorded such findings on his plats. I would guess that he did. If so, the 1600s foundation must have been an awkward problem for an organization aimed at recreating the

1776 town of George Washington, Thomas Jefferson and Patrick Henry. It seems that for many years archaeological discoveries and artifacts relating to the Middle Plantation era were simply filed and forgotten. Admittedly, recent years have seen a strong effort by the Restoration to make up for the years of neglect accorded to the pre-Williamsburg era. But a shameful amount of 1600s history was destroyed before this happened.

Take, for example, what today is known as Merchants Square. In the 1920s, when restoration began, the area of Williamsburg around the old courthouse and the Powder Magazine was the center of town. Bank, stores and offices — not to mention the courthouse — were located there. A few of the buildings dated, all or in part, to the 1700s, but many were of later vintage.

This posed a problem for the men planning to restore the town's 1776 appearance. In order to tear down what wasn't authentic and rebuild what was, the old business center of town would have to be destroyed. The early planners of the Restoration decided the solution was to build a new business center for the town — to group all the uprooted businesses and offices in the block of Duke of Gloucester Street nearest the College of William and Mary. To do this, they proceeded to tear down everything that stood there in the 1930s and replace them with modern buildings having an 1700s appearance. It seemed a splendid idea. But ...

During its first couple of centuries, Williamsburg's most important road junction was the intersection of Richmond and Jamestown Roads at College Corner. In the 1930s apparently not much thought or attention was given to checking the history and archaeology of structures that might have existed in its vicinity. Cellars and foundations were dug and brick buildings erected on both sides of the street. Admittedly, they were much more attractive than the seedy, inexpensive structures of the former business center of Williamsburg, but their construction destroyed all of the archaeological potential of the first block of Duke of Gloucester Street.

Just a few years ago, in excavations for a parking deck on the periphery of Merchants Square, modern archaeologists found traces of outbuildings indicating the nearby presence of many 1600s structures which were obliterated in the 1930s. Such findings on its outside edge lead one to wonder why someone didn't think about performing archaeological investigation of the area now known as Merchants Square, which may well have been the oldest part of town.

Then there's Tazewell Hall. History records that this was a large, successful plantation that occupied a large tract on Francis Street approximately opposite the Powder Magazine. It stood where South England Street had to run and its outbuildings occupied the site chosen for a new courthouse and the proposed Williamsburg Lodge. Also — unfortunately — John Randolph, its owner in 1776, was a Tory. This probably had nothing to do with its disposition, but for whatever reason, Tazewell Hall lost out — and there was no second best. The main house was moved to an empty lot behind the new Williamsburg Lodge and all the outbuildings and their foundations simply wiped out.

When I was a W&M freshman, CW opened the Lodge Game Room (as it was then known) to students for dancing on Sunday evenings. It was free of charge, perfect for my economic status, with music provided by, as I recall, a record player. When one tired of dancing and if he had a cooperative date, he might take her for a walk behind the Lodge where, dark, abandoned and sitting on blocks, Tazewell Hall offered shelter where a couple could sit and study the heavens.

Ultimately a well-to-do Newport News resident bought Tazewell Hall, had the historic mansion carefully taken apart, then reassembled in his city, twenty miles away.

One wonders how many modern residents or visitors realize that for more than a century there was no Duke of Gloucester Street as we know it today, running in a 99-foot-wide, ruler-straight, mile-long boulevard between William and Mary and the Colonial Capitol. The unnamed road that preceded Duke of Gloucester Street made a number of snakelike wiggles to avoid the heads of ravines which intruded upon a straight-line course. When archaeologists uncovered the site of the Bruton Parish Church building of 1674, they discovered its foundations did not line up with today's Duke of Gloucester Street. It had obviously been built to line up with the 1600s road, which ran sort of diagonally across Palace Green.

There have been other similar discoveries. In the summer of 1999, a 1600s tavern was excavated. In order to disinter its foundations, Nassau Street had to be closed and torn up. Like the original Bruton Parish Church, the tavern was not aligned with the modern Duke of Gloucester Street — a fact plainly visible to thousands who walked by the site.

I've been told that at one time there were many visible remains of 1600s structures in and around Williamsburg. Today only a few have not been obliterated by housing developments or highway construction. For example, when I was a W&M student, Jamestown Road was only two lanes wide. At the south end of the Matoaka Lake causeway, on the downstream side, the foundations of Jones' Mill — the reason the dam was built in the 1600s — could be seen. Then the road was widened, burying all traces of the colonial mill.

Some sites remain. In 1987, for instance, a 1600s structure was uncovered at Port Anne, near College Creek, off South Henry Street. A CW archaeologist said it might well have been one of the earliest home sites in Middle Plantation. Jim Knight, who prowled through the woods around town seeking traces of such habitation, told me about one such site located in the woods behind Walsingham Academy. He said it was the location of a large plantation. Sure enough, when the property was prepared for development in 1993, evidence of five houses that existed in the 1600s was discovered. Archaeologists believe they included the homes of Thomas and Philip Ludwell and commented upon the wealth of artifacts they unearthed.

The William and Mary campus provided a surprise in 1997 — and further proof of the importance of the Merchants Square area to the Middle Plantation settlement when foundations of a 1600s residence were discovered next to the Wren Building. It had to have existed before establishment of the college in 1693.

Another discovery, made by a pipeline construction crew in 1992, was the trace of a wooden palisade built at the behest of the General Assembly in 1633. Intended to protect settlers from Indian attacks, it ran between the James and York watersheds. The site located by the pipeline workers is just a couple of hundred yards west of the Division of Motor Vehicles office at the intersection of Capitol Landing Road and Merrimac Trail.

The twists and turns of the 1600s road between College Corner and the Yorktown Road at the other end of town were probably of little concern to the residents of Middle Plantation. They were undoubtedly glad to be away from the fevers and fires of Jamestown Island. However, one wonders at their reaction in the 1690s to the news that Virginia's seat of government would be moved to their Middle Plantation settlement.

In order to build an appropriately attractive capital for Virginia, largest of the colonies, the men in power at the General Assembly in Jamestown had a city plan drafted. It called for straight, orderly streets (two of them named by Royal Governor Francis Nicholson — surprise! — Francis and Nicholson). In order to create this new center of government, it can be assumed that surveyors marked out lines, then work parties filled in gullies, cut down trees and, no doubt, tore down or moved some buildings. Thus, for the first — but not last — time in its history, Williamsburg was struck by change.

One wonders if the residents of Middle Plantation protested the disruptions and destruction of their settlement, let alone the loss of their settlement's name. In the modern era, Williamsburg area residents are forever protesting this or that new development while driving around with "Welcome to Williamsburg" bumper stickers. I don't suppose the folk who lived here in the late 1600s hung banners on their wagons and saddlebags reading "Welcome to Middle Plantation."

CHAPTER TWO

The Glory Years

Middle Plantation's name was changed to Williamsburg in 1699. Soon the historic area took on much of the shape we see today. As capital of Virginia, the largest and probably most influential of the colonies, it flourished. At one end of the now straight-as-an-arrow Duke of Gloucester Street an imposing capitol building symbolized the political power centered in Williamsburg. At the opposite end, the College of William and Mary nurtured future leaders of the colony. Overlooking all of it, a royal governor endowed with the power of the English throne resided in his magnificent palace-like mansion.

Many wealthy and influential Virginians who resided on Tidewater plantations built second homes in Williamsburg in order to attend meetings of the General Assembly and participate in its social life. They probably worshipped at Bruton Parish Church, whose Church of England ritual was, if not officially so, effectively the state religion. The men gathered at Raleigh Tavern and other watering places for relaxation.

This was the fertile soil which nurtured the growth of a generation of giants, the men who saw the need for an independent America, conspired to attain it, and fought successfully to win it. Along the way, they invented a new kind of government. Chief among the leaders were names familiar to all Americans: George Washington, Thomas Jefferson and Patrick Henry. All lived in Williamsburg at one time or another, many beginning as William and Mary students, then returning later as delegates to the General Assembly.

Climax of Williamsburg's greatness came with the beginning of the American Revolution. This is the period most emphasized in history books and celebrated by Colonial Williamsburg. So much has been printed, talked and sung about that era, I'll not dwell upon it, but skip ahead to what happened after its years of fame.

A major reason that a curtain dropped on Williamsburg's glory years was geographical. The town was too close to both the James and York Rivers. South Henry Street led to Princess Anne's Port, complete with warehouses, on College Creek, a tributary of the James. Capitol Landing Road took traders to and from Queen Mary's Port on Queen's Creek, a tributary of the York. Although today these 'ports' are silted and shallow, in colonial times they were vital connections to navigable water.

This happy circumstance contributed significantly to Williamsburg's growth during the 1700s, but during the Revolutionary War that navigable water threatened the capital's security because of England's overwhelming command of the sea. Thus the General Assembly moved Virginia's capital to Richmond. (The fact that Richmond was a great deal closer to the Charlottesville home of Governor Thomas Jefferson might also have influenced the move.)

As it turned out, the change of address was a smart move. In 1781 Lord Cornwallis, Banastre Tarleton and turncoat Benedict Arnold used Britain's control of the rivers to invade and make virtually unopposed forays into eastern Virginia, including Williamsburg.

Hardly anyone is aware that in the summer of 1781, a few months before he holed up in Yorktown, Cornwallis whipped a small American army within sight of Jamestown Island, just a couple of miles from Williamsburg. Named the Battle of Green Spring, it came about when Cornwallis, marching from Richmond on his way to Portsmouth to meet supply ships, decided to cross the James River at Jamestown. Lafayette and Anthony Wayne, who had been following the English with a smaller force of Americans, decided to attack Cornwallis when half his army was across the river.

The canny English general outfoxed the Americans, pretending to row troops across the James, but actually hiding them along the banks of Powhatan Creek. (That's the small stream motorists cross on the way to the Jamestown ferry.) When the Americans marched down Green Spring Road to attack what they assumed was only a part of the English army, they were ambushed and sent packing. There's a report that some of the Americans didn't stop running until they reached Burnt Ordinary, known today as Toano. The fact that this was a rather one-sided defeat

Colonial Williamsburg Foundation

Symbolizing the return of Williamsburg's glory days are the colorfully uniformed, disciplined teenagers of Colonial Williamsburg Foundation's Fifes and Drums.

for our side may explain why the Battle of Green Spring received so little attention then and now.

Fortunately, we got revenge on Cornwallis in October, in a battle just twelve miles on the other side of Williamsburg. Cornwallis was so humiliated at being defeated at Yorktown by the Americans and French that he told everyone he was sick and sent an underling to surrender his sword for him.

By then, of course, Williamsburg was no longer capital of Virginia, but it was still in good condition. This made it possible for an engineer with the French army, which was quartered in Williamsburg after the

Battle of Yorktown, to draw a detailed map of the town. This, 'The Frenchman's Map', became a priceless tool when Colonial Williamsburg undertook to restore the town to its colonial appearance.

Stagnation

Departure of the victorious American and French armies after the victory at Yorktown, on the heels of the move of the capital to Richmond, left a vacuum in Williamsburg. Although it had a county courthouse, a small college and a mental hospital, the town lost the importance, not to mention the glamour, it had enjoyed during most of the 1700s. That's not to say it withered on the vine, but it certainly shrunk.

As the years passed, the Palace, Capitol and other structures burned down, but a relatively large number of the town's colonial buildings survived into the 1900s. Many underwent alterations, additions and/or suffered from neglect, but their continued existence was the genesis of Williamsburg's restoration.

The town achieved brief prominence again in May 1862 when a bloody battle took place on its eastern edge. That's where a Confederate army, retreating toward Richmond from the lower Peninsula, turned to fight pursuing Yankees. Most of the fighting took place in the vicinity of Quarterpath and Penniman Roads.

When the Southerners abandoned Williamsburg the next day, the town was occupied by Northern forces. This was a situation which more or less continued during the remainder of the War Between the States, although the town was never held in great strength. Men serving in the James City cavalry, a company in the Fifth Virginia Cavalry — which included many Williamsburg men — found it relatively easy to sneak into town for occasional visits to their families.

In September 1862 the Wren Building, which was fire-prone throughout its long history, was allegedly set ablaze by Yankee soldiers. Gutted, it was a crushing blow to William and Mary, because it had housed students, classrooms, library and dining hall. Because of the fire, the difficulties of Reconstruction and economic woes, the college barely survived the last half of the 1800s.

By the beginning of the 1900s, Williamsburg's decline had become a slide into oblivion. Without the presence of Eastern State Hospital, it might have dried up and blown away, for its role as county seat was not enough to support a mile-long Main Street. Its population dropped to less than a thousand and county residents began looking elsewhere for a focal point. In the early 1900s, Toano was vying with Williamsburg for leadership in this part of the Peninsula — and Toano was winning.

In spite of — or because of — its decline in importance, decreasing population and bucolic atmosphere, Williamsburg's people developed intense love and loyalty to their hometown and deep respect for its history. Their achievements in the years before the advent of Mr. Rockefeller, despite a lack of wealth and/or numbers, were praiseworthy.

At the top of the list is the APVA — the Association for the Preservation of Virginia Antiquities. Don't let the awkward name fool you. This was — and remains — an extraordinary organization, founded in Williamsburg by its women. It can boast a long list of achievements, not the least the fact that it took the first step in the ultimate restoration of its historic area. (Today it's known as APVA Preservation Virginia.)

Cynthia Beverley Tucker Coleman organized the APVA in January 1889 in the Coleman home on Nicholson Street, known today as the Tayloe House. The new organization's first success was in saving the Powder Magazine, which had been turned into a stable. After purchasing and repairing the structure, the APVA used it as a museum to display a scattering of artifacts. Later it bought the site of the colonial capitol at the eastern end of Duke of Gloucester Street. In 1893, the APVA acquired more than 20 acres around the old church tower at Jamestown and protected it from damaging encroachment. Although the U.S. Park Service today owns the remainder of Jamestown Island, the APVA retains ownership of 20-plus acres.

There were other modest efforts at preservation of historic buildings by residents. Mary Jeffrey Galt, a co-founder of the APVA, bought and protected the site of what was believed to have been the local jail. John Garland Pollard, who later became a governor of Virginia, rescued the John Blair House on Duke of Gloucester Street and another local resident bought and restored the Peyton Randolph House.

Vernon Geddy was not among those with the means to purchase and preserve old buildings, but he provided something even more important: a vivid picture of what it was like to live in Williamsburg during the late 1800s and early 1900s, and particularly of the early years of the Restoration and its founders.

The Preacher With a Dream

The Reverend Dr. W.A.R. Goodwin came to Williamsburg in 1903 as a youthful rector of Bruton Parish Church. He discovered that the old church had been subjected to a number of changes over the years. In fact, the pews faced exactly the opposite of their original direction. With Jamestown's 300th anniversary only four years off, Goodwin decided to do what he could to restore the church to its colonial appearance.

There's some question as to what motivated the young minister to become interested in historic restoration. In later years he told Geddy that he read a book as a young boy that inspired his interest. And during his ministry, he undoubtedly learned of and met some of the local people who, recognizing the historic importance of the town, made modest attempts to preserve some of its surviving colonial buildings. Beyond

The Reverend William Archer Rutherfoord Goodwin (left) *and John D. Rockefeller, Jr. This is an often-used photograph, and rightly so, for it is the best and most symbolic picture of the two men responsible for the creation of Colonial Williamsburg.*

Colonial Williamsburg Foundation

that, for whatever reason, Goodwin's interest grew into an obsession, an impossible dream: to turn back Williamsburg's clock.

Goodwin was not simply a dreamer. He had a unique gift — the ability to make others see his dream. As Geddy put it, "The Doctor [his name for Goodwin] was one of those men who could sell ice to Eskimos." And as his record shows, he proved it.

He interested enough people in his plans for Bruton Parish Church to have it restored in time for the 1907 Jamestown celebration. Then, in 1909, he moved to a church in Rochester, N.Y. He might have remained there, except for a change in William and Mary's administration. In 1919, Dr. J.A.C. Chandler succeeded Dr. Lyon G. Tyler as its president.

Chandler, a long time friend and admirer of Goodwin — and like the minister, also a man with vision — persuaded Goodwin to return to Williamsburg in 1923. Chandler's enticement lay in the college jobs — and challenge — he offered Goodwin. Professor of religious education was part of the package, but what really interested the rector was the prospect of raising funds for a W&M expansion program envisioned by Chandler. Today Goodwin's position at the college would probably be described as director of development. (Subsequently he again became rector of Bruton Parish Church.)

The duo of Chandler and Goodwin became a winning combination, for they launched the college's first-ever large-scale building program. That's when the Phi Beta Kappa Society entered the picture. One of the college's great needs was for an auditorium. Chandler and Goodwin hit upon the idea of using the 150th anniversary of the founding of Phi Beta Kappa at W&M — which would take place in 1926 — as a vehicle to raise money for an auditorium.

Phi Beta Kappa – Key to a Kingdom

Upon his return to Williamsburg in 1923, Goodwin had expressed deep concern over the decline of the town. According to CW's 1988 publication, *Williamsburg Before and After,*

> Goodwin crusaded to preserve and reconstruct Williamsburg, believing that the town provided an introduction to the history of colonial Virginia and, indeed, of colonial America as well. He was sure that the

> public buildings could be made to serve as memorials, recalling to people's minds the events and principles that culminated in the establishment of the Federal Republic. ... Goodwin continued seeking to interest various philanthropists in the total restoration of the colonial town by pointing out that Williamsburg was the one colonial city left that had not been obliterated or swallowed up by burgeoning urban growth and whose restoration was feasible. Other benefactors had preserved books, paintings and single houses, but the rector observed that "no man has yet had the vision and courage to preserve a colonial village, and Williamsburg is the one remaining colonial village any man could buy".
>
> The rector appealed to several members of the Ford family for support of his restoration dream. Henry Ford had already saved the Wayside Inn in South Sudbury, Massachusetts. His Greenfield Village in Dearborn, Michigan, was yet to come.

Although his request to Ford was rejected and he received polite interest but little tangible support from other prospective benefactors, Goodwin persisted. Then, almost by accident, his campaign for funds for a Phi Beta Kappa Memorial Hall became the springboard to Rockefeller's millions.

In 1924 Goodwin spoke before the New York City chapter of the Phi Beta Kappa Society on behalf of the proposed memorial auditorium. Rockefeller was in the audience and contributed substantially to the project. Goodwin invited him to visit Williamsburg. Rockefeller did so when in Tidewater with his family and Goodwin provided them with a tour of the town.

When Phi Beta Kappa Hall was dedicated in 1926, Rockefeller was among the honored guests. Goodwin was able to spend some time with him, show him many of the town's 1700s buildings, and begin to work his magic. At the end of his visit, Rockefeller said the opportunity to restore the colonial community and keep it free from incongruous surroundings was irresistible. He authorized Goodwin to engage an architect to prepare preliminary drawings showing what a restored Williamsburg might look like.

Rockefeller's appreciation of Williamsburg was close to that of Goodwin. Both recognized the town's historical importance, not only because of its many surviving structures, but also because of its value as a symbol of America's successful struggle for independence.

In Rockefeller's own words, the restoration of Williamsburg "offered an opportunity to restore a complete area entirely free from alien or inharmonious surroundings as well as to preserve the beauty and charm of the old buildings and gardens of the city and its historic significance. Thus it made a unique and irresistible appeal. As the work progressed, I have come to feel that perhaps an even greater value is the lesson that it teaches of the patriotism, high purpose and unselfish devotion of our forefathers to the common good."

In describing Rockefeller's generosity, Goodwin said that nothing will "prove more lasting, illuminating, and inspiring than what he has done, through the restoration of colonial Williamsburg, to wed truth and beauty ..."

The Reverend Dr. Goodwin is credited with creating the vision of a restored Williamsburg and persuading Mr. Rockefeller to provide the funds that made his dream come true. Granted, Goodwin deserves a huge amount of praise for his role, but there's one factor few people stop to consider: If some William and Mary students hadn't established the Phi Beta Kappa Society back in 1776, it's possible that the restoration of Williamsburg might have remained nothing but the pipe dream of a small town preacher.

My God, They've Sold the Town

That was the opening line of a poem written by local character Jack Hundley in 1928. It would have been more accurate if he'd written, 'My God, they've *bought* the town,' for he composed the poem after learning with his neighbors that John D. Rockefeller, Jr. had anonymously donated more than two million dollars — an unimaginable sum in those days — to purchase scores of properties within Williamsburg's historic area.

Until that town meeting on June 12, 1928, Williamsburg people had long been agog over the activities of the rector of Bruton Parish Church. For more than a year, with the help of attorney Vernon Geddy, the Reverend Dr. Goodwin had been buying houses, buildings and lots in the oldest parts of Williamsburg. The Episcopal clergyman did not have the kind of wealth to spend money like that, so everyone wanted to know where he was getting the funds.

Geddy recalled, "When the Doctor retained me to search titles and write contracts, he told me the source of the money was strictly confidential and I respected that. I avoided any speculation, but you couldn't live here and not hear some wild guesses. Henry Ford was a leading candidate.

"Working closely with the Doctor and with his secretary, I sometimes heard things that perhaps he intended me to hear. For instance, once or twice I heard him refer to 'his partners', which of course was very misleading. In later years, when I brought this up, he explained that he was not lying, that he considered both Mr. and Mrs. Rockefeller as his benefactors. He was a pretty smart man."

Geddy said Goodwin proved how smart he was when, knowing that his purchases of Williamsburg property would incite the curiosity of news media, he called upon the publishers of the area's leading newspapers — *Richmond Times-Dispatch*, *Richmond News Leader*, *Norfolk Virginian-Pilot* and *Newport News Daily Press* — to seek their cooperation. He outlined his dream of recreating the Williamsburg of 1776 and explained that he intended to purchase as much of the historic property as possible, but that if word got out, prices would escalate and probably prevent fulfillment of the project.

Unlike what might happen in today's unprincipled media circus, Goodwin obtained full cooperation from the newspapers. They waited until the 1928 public meeting to report that Mr. Rockefeller was donor of the funds for restoring Williamsburg. That public meeting became necessary when Goodwin sought arrangements for use of city property. Residents voted 150 to 5 to support the town council in granting Goodwin's requests. That approval and enthusiasm was reflected in the first of what became Jack Hundley's three-part poem:

My God, they've sold the town,
My God, they've sold the town!
They've sold the Powder Horn,
The schoolhouse and the lawn,
It is the tale they've sold the jail
And the streets we walk upon.
They've sold the Courthouse Green,
I daresay all the people,

They'll sell the church, the vestry too,
And even so the steeple.
The streets will all come up,
The poles will all come down,
So take it from me, stranger,
It's going to be some town.

Hundley never pretended to be a Nostradamus, but he was right as far as he went. However, when he wrote that tiny Williamsburg would become 'some town', he didn't know that it would ultimately grow as it has. In their wildest dreams, none of the 155 people who voted at that 1928 meeting could have imagined that the local population would exceed 60,000 by the end of the century.

Depression? What's That?

Few Americans are still alive who remember the Great Depression of the 1930s, but like Pearl Harbor, it left a permanent, irrevocable memory on those who experienced it. Almost everyone was affected one way or another throughout our nation. Millions of men and women lost their jobs.

Except in Williamsburg that is, where the immense building program undertaken by CW created prosperity and permanently changed the town's demographics. As America's economy crashed after the Wall Street collapse of 1929, Mr. Rockefeller pumped money into restoring and rebuilding 1776 Williamsburg. There were jobs aplenty at every level of construction and no unemployment even among the less skilled. This is not to say there wasn't also a demand for white collar professionals. Men with architectural, engineering or other professional qualifications arrived from New York, Boston and points north.

Soon enough, the local supply of labor dried up. Workers and artisans began commuting from nearby communities like Newport News, Hampton and Gloucester. Before long, men — with their families — came from homes farther afield. Socially and economically, this influx stood the town on its ear. Williamsburg families, most of them with long-standing local roots, were soon outnumbered by newcomers

— Yankees, West Virginians, Carolinians, even invaders from nearby Hampton Roads communities.

Families which had been mired in low-income jobs for generations became more affluent. Suddenly, refined older ladies of Williamsburg had to rub shoulders with what they privately called 'white trash' when they went shopping — and when the good ol' boys wanted to buy their Virginia Gentleman bourbon at the state-controlled store, they had to stand in line with po' whites and others to get it.

That sort of inconvenience didn't trouble newcomers like A.T. 'Red' Vaughan, who came from a tobacco farm in Southside Virginia. He arrived in Williamsburg at the age of 24 in 1927, and became one of the first out-of-towners to work on the restoration, which was just beginning. His specialty was masonry, which led him ultimately to supervising all bricklaying — a major function in restoring and rebuilding structures and sidewalks in the historic area. That's because colonial builders, with no concrete or native rocks available, built with bricks made from the clay which abounds on the Peninsula.

Vernon Geddy told me something about the 1700s source of bricks in Williamsburg. In the 1940s, when the Restoration began planning a visitor information and reception center, I asked him if it was true that it would be built on the other side of the railroad tracks. He gave me an embarrassed grin as he nodded. "It's going right where the race track used to be." Race track? I'd never heard of it. He explained, "Our researchers told me they held horse races there in colonial days." Then he added, "They also told me that most of the bricks they used in building the Palace and the Capitol were made in that area because it had good clay."

Red Vaughan estimated that more than 15 million bricks went into the restoration. He said bricklaying for CW was like bricklaying nowhere else. To begin with, Red believed he was on a single job longer than any other bricklayer in America, because "it was the longest bricklaying job that ever came along". He said all of the many bricklayers who worked for him had to learn their trade all over again because Williamsburg's handmade bricks, unlike modern machine-made bricks, were not consistent in size. And his men had to produce neat Flemish or English bond, of which all restorations were made. The most difficult jobs, Vaughan said, were the huge fireplaces typical of 1700s houses and, hardest of all, erecting brick arches that are common in restored buildings.

Vaughan achieved a different degree of local fame as the father of six of the town's best-looking girls. On a warm day, when they sat on the steps of their South Boundary Street home — just a couple of doors from Tyler Hall — a veritable parade of W&M men found reasons to take a walk in that direction.

Bill Stout was a second-generation resident who built a thriving lawnmower business on old Route 168, now Rochambeau Road. He arrived with his family from West Virginia during the 1930s. "Coal mines shut down, so there weren't no jobs where we lived, not much

Courtesy of Joyce Vaughan Robertson

A.T. 'Red' Vaughan not only raised the brick walls of scores of restored and reconstructed colonial structures, he raised beautiful daughters, too.

to eat, either," he said. "A cousin of ours told Pa he could get work here, so we came."

Bill, admittedly no genius in school, was an honest, conscientious hard worker, much like Dudley Waltrip. Dudley grew up on a small farm in the Five Forks area. He told me he didn't get past fourth grade in school, that he went to work as a teen. After a spell of working for others, he obtained a mule and what he called a 'pan' and hired himself out to contractors who needed excavation work.

If the Waltrip name is prominent in Williamsburg today, it's not because anyone anointed them. They earned their way. I remember a beautiful, sunny Memorial Day a few years ago when I drove over to Dudley's home to ask if he wanted to do some fishing. He knew more about College Creek than any man alive and was kind enough to share some of that knowledge with me.

He wasn't home. His wife Mary told me he and 'the boys' were down at the airport, which the Waltrips built. I went there to see what he was up to and found Dudley, then in his 70s, working with a shovel, helping sons Larry and Timmy and grandson Timmy Two to build a new taxiway. It was proof, if proof was needed, that Waltrips weren't afraid to work. That's why they were successful.

Henry Branscome's story was not exactly like the Waltrips', but it followed the same sort of pattern, with a major exception. Branscome, originally from Newport News, was blessed with a remarkable memory, not only for names and faces, but for equipment, job openings and opportunities. One time I teased him about the wealth he acquired and he told me, "The Lord blessed me with the ability to find cheap and sell dear." Henry repaid his debt to the Lord by building and donating a church to his religious sect.

Another man who came here from Newport News was Jimmy Maloney, who arrived in the 1930s, learned something about making pottery, and established his own kiln on Route 60 in Lightfoot in 1938. Starting on the proverbial shoestring, his hard work and brilliant merchandising made his Williamsburg Pottery into Virginia's largest retail operation in one location. For many years it has ranked as a major attraction for visitors.

In the 1950s I wrote a feature story about Jimmy for the *Times-Dispatch*. He never forgot it. Many years later, while threading my way through the crowds that besieged the Pottery, I caught sight of him off to one side watching the flow of people. None of the hundreds of shoppers swarming around Jimmy would ever have identified him as the multi-millionaire who had created this incredible retail mecca, for he was attired — as usual — in scruffy jeans, nondescript shirt, tennis shoes and a baseball cap.

Newport News Daily Press

Jimmy Maloney (right) *didn't build a better mousetrap, he built a hugely successful way to merchandise his products at the Williamsburg Pottery.*

I stopped to speak to him — nothing of great consequence, just a friendly exchange. As I left him, he said something to the effect, "It sure is nice talking to somebody who isn't asking me to give money to something or other."

There was something wistful about that parting shot. Jimmy anonymously contributed large amounts to a number of worthwhile causes but perhaps he wondered whether folks liked him or his money. No matter. He made a huge impact on our area.

It would be difficult — impossible, actually — to measure what the influx of these people did to change Williamsburg. In addition to families like the Branscomes, Maloneys, Stouts, Vaughans and Waltrips, there were many, many more. Their presence was a major force in shaping the Williamsburg that developed in the latter half of the 1900s.

Last House Standing

When Goodwin began buying Williamsburg property in 1927, he did all of the negotiating, but Geddy searched the titles, wrote contracts and handled all other legal aspects of the purchases which were made in the name of Williamsburg Holding Corporation. Only 29 years old when he began the job, Geddy often referred to the amount of work he accomplished and the sheer excitement he experienced during that period when no one knew the source of the huge amounts of money Goodwin was spending. "When the Doctor arranged a sale, he wanted to close it as soon as possible. Sometimes that meant burning the midnight oil."

He said Goodwin began his purchases with properties already listed for sale. After that the minister dealt with owners who had to be persuaded in one way or another that selling to the Doctor would be beneficial. In cases that involved surviving 1700s structures, one of his most successful approaches was to offer the owner life rights to his property. This created additional work for Geddy, because a contract had to be written to detail responsibilities for items such as taxes and maintenance.

There's no doubt that Geddy relished working with the Doctor. His admiration for Goodwin showed in almost every reference he ever made to the Episcopal minister, whom he first knew as a nine-year-old in a Sunday school class. By the time the Doctor put him to work in 1927, Geddy was serving as a member of the Bruton Parish vestry.

Not everyone in Williamsburg shared Geddy's unbounded admiration of Goodwin, for the minister was recalled with bitterness by some folks whose parents or grandparents sold their homes to him. There were not many such voices and they will not be identified here, but they came from both white and black sources.

That's something not many modern residents realize: In the early years of the 1900s, right up to the restoration, Williamsburg was an integrated community. Black and white families lived in the same neighborhoods. Lenny Graves, who for many years operated a men's clothing store, talked of his black childhood playmate, Fred Epps, Jr. The Epps family was widely known and respected in Williamsburg. Fred Sr. worked at the post office and sang in a quartet that entertained us on many occasions. Fred Jr. became a captain in the Williamsburg Lodge Dining Room. His brother Warren was a doorman at the Inn.

The complaints about Goodwin's purchases mostly stemmed from the sales prices awarded in those early days — and came mainly from descendents of folks who had limited incomes at the time. If the criticisms are true, the Episcopal minister apparently did not always play his game on a level field, that he took advantage of people not equipped, either financially or educationally, to counter his persuasive arguments. Thus they might occasionally have sold their properties for less than they could have received had they held out for more.

Geddy, like most of Goodwin's supporters, brushed off such complaints. "The Doctor was an honest man," he said, "and always did the best he could, but there will always be people who think they should have received more money."

He admitted that those who were first to sell their homes received lower prices than home owners who waited. "When the Doctor began buying properties, he went first for those listed for sale and met the asking price. Then prices began to rise. That's the nature of an open market." And rise they did.

As this is being written, CW either owns outright or controls every property within the Historic Area except the 1858 Bowden-Armistead House, which sits on an acre lot on Nassau Street between Duke of Gloucester and Prince George Streets. It is the last house standing, so to speak, so it's probably worth much more today than the two million dollars the Reverend Dr. Goodwin spent for all the homes he bought in 1927. One veteran Williamsburg Realtor said the city assessed it at $883,000 in 2005, but that its real value is probably in the multi-millions.

The Bowden-Armistead House, privately owned, is the only property in the historic area of Williamsburg which is not owned or controlled by Colonial Williamsburg Foundation or the City of Williamsburg. It is located at the corner of Duke of Gloucester and Nassau Streets.

Chapter Three

Welcome to Williamsburg, Stranger

My decision to leave home and travel to Williamsburg was triggered by Dr. Albert DeLisle, an assistant professor of biology at W&M. A neighbor of ours when he was a youth in South Hadley Falls, DeLisle had returned to his hometown to recruit boys for something called the War Work Program at William and Mary. He sought young men with the desire and grades, but not the money, for college and offered them an opportunity to work their way through. Although I was two years out of high school, he assured me I was qualified. With the promise of enrollment in the Naval Reserve, which would protect me from the immediacy of the draft and offer the possibility of an officer's commission, I signed up.

I was twenty years old. Most of the other young men who entered the War Work Program were eighteen, some only seventeen. I can't recall all of the boys DeLisle signed up from the South Hadley–Springfield area of Massachusetts, but among them were two sets of brothers — the Johnstons and Porters — and John Daley, Pat Haggerty, Harry Tanzer and Bob Whitman.

Early in the morning of July 6, 1942, in Holyoke, Massachusetts, I boarded the southbound *Montrealer*, a New Haven train that ran between Montreal and Washington. One old suitcase held my entire wardrobe and my wallet contained about $22. Everything else I'd earned as a toolgrinder at Pratt & Whitney Aircraft I left with my mother and brother.

I was on my way to a town about which I knew nothing except that it was somewhere in Virginia and was the home of the College of William and Mary. I knew only that its football team had come to New England the previous autumn and beaten Dartmouth, which in those days was a huge upset.

Of one thing I was absolutely sure: I wanted desperately to get a college education. During the spring of 1942 I attended evening classes at American International College in Springfield. The fact that it would take at least eight years to earn a degree was daunting.

In Washington, jammed with uniformed service men, I squeezed aboard a crowded coach on the Richmond, Fredericksburg & Potomac Railroad. Some hours later, having become acquainted with the muggy heat of Virginia's Tidewater, I was deposited on a platform at Broad Street Station in Richmond. To get from there to Williamsburg, it was necessary to travel across town to the Main Street Station and a connection on the Chesapeake and Ohio Railway. I found myself with a small group of young men who also sought to reach Williamsburg. We split the cost of a taxi and caught an early evening train. It was still daylight when we arrived in Williamsburg.

Amid the buzz, laughter and talk of people crowding the platform, I heard a man's voice booming out. It took only a few moments to realize he was calling for me in a mountain drawl that thoroughly butchered my French Canadian name. He towered over me, a big, rawboned guy. I asked if he was calling me.

"Daggone!" he grinned. "Didn't know how to say yore name. Ah'm Rube McCray. Got a car ovah heah, lemme he'p you with yore bag an' Ah'll get you to yore dormitory." I didn't know it at the time, but Rube McCray was an assistant to football coach Carl Voyles, whom he later succeeded.

That was my welcome to Williamsburg and William and Mary. I'll never forget it. Or Rube McCray.

TNT in Shoes, Detonators in Hands, Nothing in Pockets

If hardly anyone else recalls William and Mary's short-lived War Work Program of 1942 and if college records on the subject are scanty and inaccurate, it is understandable. The War Work Program was not among William and Mary's most illustrious moments.

On its face the program seemed noble and altruistic, for it offered penniless young men an opportunity to work their way through college. Good intentions undoubtedly played a part, but so did pure expediency, a desperate effort to flesh out depleted male enrollment. Hastily staged and inadequately planned, it began in July 1942 and blundered its way to oblivion in December of the same year.

The War Work Program might have become William and Mary's most ignominious failure since 1693 except for Vernon Geddy, who provided a stroke of luck which bailed out the college and retrieved some of the War Work boys from its wreckage. Almost overnight the War Work Program became Work Study. War Work was swept under the rug so abruptly and with such finality that one suspects the college wished it had never happened.

Ex-War Workers share a number of distinctions. We constituted the largest group of non-athletes ever recruited by W&M. They were the direct cause of a change in the employment requirements of the U.S. Civil Service Commission. We were sent by William and Mary to jobs that required us to work literally ankle deep in TNT surrounded by thousands of tons of high explosives and to install firing mechanisms in secret, sensitive magnetic mines capable of blowing ships in half. And we became, unwittingly, charter members of W&M's very successful Work Study Program.

In the spring of 1942 the war had eroded male enrollment and dried up the flow of applications from men for admission to the fall term. President John Stewart Bryan, then in the final months of his tenure, solicited suggestions for ways to avoid empty dormitories. Dr. Sharvy Umbeck, professor of sociology and tennis coach (later president of Knox College), proposed a solution. Rapidly expanding defense installations in the area were desperate for help. His idea, based upon a program at the University of Chicago, was to seek qualified young men willing to work their way through college, place them in jobs and enroll them as part-time students. From their earnings they could pay weekly installments on room, board and tuition.

The prospect of helping deserving young men obtain an education and contribute to the war effort while filling a college need was so attractive that Bryan bought it. But Umbeck, committed to a summer job in Chicago, was not available to implement it. The project landed in the lap of economics professor Hibbert D. Corey. Years later he told me he had neither solicited nor welcomed the assignment. He recalled that he was about fifth choice, that the first four nominees had managed to find excuses to avoid the task. He could not. "And by the time Mr. Bryan got down to me it was almost the end of May. I had to line up jobs and find boys in time to start the program July 1st. I had no idea how little preparation had been done."

Under the circumstances, Corey probably performed as well as anyone. He lined up jobs easily enough, for the Naval Mine Depot (now Naval Weapons Station) at Yorktown promised to hire every young man Corey could send there. Finding enough young men to enroll in the program in the four or five weeks remaining to him was a more difficult proposition. Although he sent news releases to newspapers, wire services and radio stations, Corey realized that personal solicitation was necessary. The young men would have to be recruited.

Corey turned to an expert for help. Accordingly, Rube McCray, chief recruiter of football players, organized and mounted a recruiting drive. He sent faculty and staff members on the road following final exams in early June. DeLisle was the most productive recruiter. He signed up boys in Danville, Virginia; Frederick, Maryland; and Johnson City, Tennessee, then produced a twelve-man contingent from Massachusetts.

Recruiters worked through high school principals and teachers to identify recent graduates with the qualifications and desire, but not the funds, to attend college. A visit to the boys and their parents followed. If the prospect was of draft age, he was told he could enlist in an Army or Navy reserve program. Altogether it was an attractive and challenging offer.

If the recruiters painted a rosy, optimistic picture of the War Work Program, it was not their fault. They didn't know that planning for the program was virtually non-existent, that no one had anticipated the problems that would arise. For example, many of the boys being enrolled, particularly those from rural Virginia with its eleven-year school programs, were seventeen, some only sixteen. But minimum age for Civil Service employment at the Naval Mine Depot was eighteen!

Supported by an urgent plea from the depot's commanding officer, Corey somehow managed to cut through Washington's bureaucratic red tape. The Civil Service Commission enacted an emergency rule lowering minimum Civil Service age to seventeen for the duration of the war.

Corey was in the midst of trying to solve the many problems — and running into new ones — when the boys began to arrive. Near the end of June 1942, Bill Holland of Surry County crossed on the Jamestown

Ferry and checked into Tyler Hall. He was the first War Worker. Most of the rest of us arrived in the first two weeks of July. To the credit of Hib Corey and Rube McCray, almost every one of us was met at the train or bus station by a college representative.

This kind of welcome gave the boys the impression that William and Mary was glad they had come. It was a state of mind which helped us survive the disillusions that followed. Housing, for instance. The first arrivals were assigned to rooms in Tyler Hall on the basis of double the designed occupancy. Later arrivals were assigned space in the attic of Old Dominion Hall, others sent to the upper floor of the old infirmary, or to rooms over the Corner Greek's, the A&P and other unused corners of the war-crowded town.

No one knows exactly how many young men ultimately enrolled in the War Work Program. If a roster was ever compiled, it disappeared. Former War Workers agree that the number was well over 200, possibly close to 300, but attrition began immediately. Some of the boys packed and left a few days after arriving.

Homesickness and overcrowding might have caused some to leave, but there were other reasons, not the least of which was food. In theory the War Workers were to be fed in the college dining hall, but in practice we had to use our scanty cash resources and weekly pay to supplement the fare. W&M's dining establishment, short of both staff and food because of the war, never fed us adequately. The bagged lunches issued each morning to carry to work were particularly grim — occasionally consisting of cheese of obscure ancestry between two slices of stale bread tinged with mold.

A bitter disappointment was the discovery we would not start classes until September. Many, if not most, arrived under the impression that we would enroll in summer session. Instead we were expected to work full time at college-assigned jobs, pay for rooms, board and transportation, and make weekly payments toward full tuition. That became even more galling when we discovered we probably could have earned more by getting (or remaining in) jobs at home.

Most were sent to the Naval Mine Depot. After filling out a simple form, being fingerprinted and given a cursory physical examination, we were supposed to show our job qualifications by carrying a 60-pound weight 12 feet. For many of the boys, this requirement had to be overlooked. Then we were issued identification badges with the lowest of all Civil Service classifications: Second Class Laborer.

Except for a handful of youths sent to other employers — the 16-year-olds, for instance, worked on a pipeline construction project — the War Workers immediately became intimate with TNT, the depot's chief stock in trade. It came in 58-pound wooden boxes — 50 pounds of explosive in an 8-pound container 12 inches wide, 19 inches long and 10 inches high. During most of the hot, humid summer of 1942 we unloaded TNT from scores of boxcars which glutted the railroad tracks, including several temporary sidings, within the depot.

TNT boxes were not skid-loaded. There were no fork lifts. Every box was manhandled — tens of thousands of them — one at a time. Because the depot had run out of magazine storage, the War Workers stacked the boxes 20 layers high in huge piles on what had been a World War I Naval Air Station.

Many of the hastily fabricated boxes leaked. Others fell apart in handling or dropped and burst open. As a result, we worked upon a thick carpet of what looked and felt like yellow soap powder, except it was TNT. It filled our shoes like beach sand and impregnated our hair, skin and clothing. We became accustomed to it. Too accustomed. In hiding places thoughtfully built into the vast stacks of TNT, some of the boys thoughtlessly took cigarette breaks!

War Workers were often drafted from the TNT crews to perform more onerous tasks. One hellish job required the use of live steam to remove caked TNT from obsolete World War I depth charges. This took place on a concrete apron at P-2, a small building at the bottom of an artificial hollow. Working there with a steam hose on a 90- or 100-degree day was an experience not easily forgotten. (The old TNT was unstable. Less than a year later P-2 vanished in an explosion.)

Without doubt the most unsavory assignment given the War Workers was the handling of an explosive known as Ammonium Picric. After working with the vile stuff for an hour or two the boys turned yellow — clothing, skin and hair. At first it was amusing to discover it also caused urine to turn bright orange. The jaundiced look and gaudy excretion persisted for several days.

Eventually we cleaned up the depot's backlog of TNT boxcars and were transferred to the Mine Assembly Plant — and were not reassured to see that this establishment was surrounded on all sides by a towering artificial hill, not to protect the plant, but to protect the rest of the depot in case of an explosion. Hundreds of contact and magnetic mines, each capable of destroying a ship, arrived at Mine Assembly fully loaded with TNT. The task of the teenagers from William and Mary was to make them operational. This involved installation of the firing components — magnetic sensing devices, booster charges, detonators. A wire wrongly connected or a short circuit would have abruptly terminated the War Work Program.

A perfect example of the program's inept administration was the astounding statement, made in a report submitted to incoming W&M President John E. Pomfret in September 1942, that the boys' work at the depot was 'of a non-hazardous nature'!

That incredible SNAFU was emblematic of the way in which the college lost touch with realities of the War Workers' situation. Although tanned and toughened by their summer of grueling labor, the boys had fallen into desperate financial straits. Their pay as second class laborers was simply too low to meet both living expenses and tuition payments.

Nevertheless, in September almost 200 surviving War Workers were permitted to register for classes. (Many of us were then taken to Richmond and enrolled in the Naval Reserve V-12 program.) About half were assigned to work Mondays, Wednesdays and Fridays, the remainder Tuesdays, Thursdays and Saturdays. On non-working days, we attended classes (there were Saturday classes in those days). Most carried two three-hour courses and a five-hour science. We were granted one hour of physical education credit in recognition of our exertions at the depot. Thus we could earn 12 semester hours of credit. Normal load was 15 hours.

Being away from campus three days a week, carrying a demanding academic load, and possessing little spending money limited our participation in normal undergraduate activities. Our self-esteem was not enhanced when, grubby and grimy after our 10-hour work day, we were unloaded from trucks or buses at College Corner in full view of coeds walking to and from the dining hall and post office.

We were caught in an economic squeeze. Working only three days cut our income, already insufficient, nearly in half. War Workers, particularly out-of-staters facing higher tuition charges, fell farther and farther in debt to the College.

We were also squeezed between the need for study time and the physical demands of our jobs. We were soon leaving and returning to campus in the dark. As the weather became colder and wetter, our work became an ordeal. If we were not shivering in the unheated Mine Assembly Plant, we were outdoors performing heavy physical labor like loading or unloading flatcars full of mine anchors. After days like this it was difficult for many of us stay awake long enough to prepare for the next day's classes.

It is not surprising that morale plummeted and we lost our motivation. Absenteeism became a serious problem at the depot and more and more boys dropped out. By Thanksgiving the War Work Program had all but disintegrated. But just then, an unexpected rescuer materialized.

Dr. Pomfret had taken office as president September 1st. He immediately put Dr. Umbeck, who had returned from the University of Chicago and was originator of the War Work idea, in charge of the program. They quickly became aware of the chaos they had inherited. Dr. Pomfret liked the basic idea, but realized the employment arrangement with the Naval Mine Depot was unsatisfactory. He and Umbeck agreed the only way to save the program was to find better jobs for the boys. That wasn't easy.

As the fall term progressed, some War Workers were transferred to more suitable jobs. Dick Duncan and Fred Flanary went to work as shoe salesmen at Casey's Department Store. Harmon Hoffman became an usher at the Williamsburg Theater. Tommy Smith and Johnny Warner donned the white jackets of dining hall waiters and played trombone and trumpet, respectively, in the college dance band.

These were steps in the right direction, but of themselves would have been too little and too late except for a bridge game which took place in the late fall of 1942. It involved Vernon and Carrie Cole Geddy and Jack and Sarah Pomfret. Almost overnight War Workers discovered that we were part of something called the Work Study Program. War Work died quietly and mercifully.

A Student Could Enjoy the Town

In spite of everything, even as virtually penniless, physically exhausted young men, War Workers became aware of the physical beauties of Williamsburg's historic area, for by the summer of 1942 much of the restoration had been completed. During freshman orientation in early September, we were given guided tours of the restored area, including visits inside the major buildings.

When we had time, some extra cash and could finagle a date with one of the coeds attending summer school, we'd walk down Duke of Gloucester Street in the evening. Our destination was often Chowning's Tavern, a college hangout in those days. If one were so inclined, he could purchase a pitcher of beer for twenty-five cents and make it last all evening.

Although steeped in the history of Massachusetts with its Pilgrims and Plymouth Rock, I began to understand and appreciate Williamsburg and its history. This wasn't only because of the beauty of the restored area or the realization that I had lucked out in landing in a great college town. It was also due to the attitude of townspeople. It's difficult to document, but even across more than sixty years, I can recall an atmosphere of friendliness and tolerance.

This was a positive development, of course, but it didn't solve the basic problem confronting War Workers. Although we closed ranks during the fall of 1942 and successfully elected two members of our group president and vice president of the freshman class, that was the only highlight. We knew that our lack of income threatened to end our college careers. Then a miracle occurred. In December I discovered that Colonial Williamsburg would make it possible for me — and 15 other War Workers — to remain in school. I almost exploded with gratitude.

The vehicle for this huge stroke of fortune was the Travis House.

The Marvelous Travis House

The Travis House was an authentic Eighteenth Century dwelling originally located on Francis Street on the grounds of Eastern State Hospital. In the 1930s CW moved it to Duke of Gloucester Street opposite Palace Green and across from the James Geddy House. There it rested, somewhat uneasily, upon the foundations of the John Greenhow House, a colonial structure which no longer existed.

The Restoration installed a kitchen in the basement and began operating Travis House as a restaurant. Food was delivered to the first floor in a dumbwaiter fitted into a tiny service area. Three dining rooms

Colonial Williamsburg Foundation

The Travis House in 1943, when it was used as a restaurant on Duke of Gloucester Street on the current site of the John Greenhow House opposite the James Geddy House. This location was not historically accurate. It was later returned to its original site at the corner of Francis and South Henry Streets.

provided a seating capacity of about 60. In good weather, garden tables seated another 20 or 30 diners.

Despite its lack of size and inefficient operating arrangements, in the late 1930s Travis House became Williamsburg's leading restaurant. Unfortunately, the onset of World War II forced it to close because of lack of employees. Service workers like waiters flocked to higher-paying jobs at the Newport News shipyard and other war-related businesses on the Peninsula.

Without Travis House, the town suffered from a dearth of fine dining during the early war years. The Williamsburg Inn had closed its dining room and become housing for military and naval families. The Lodge and other local restaurants were overwhelmed, handicapped by both a shortage of help and food.

In the fall of 1942, John D. Green, general manager of CW's hotel and restaurant operations, was told to reopen the Travis House. The order came from CW President Kenneth Chorley, who was in his New York office. When Green ran into difficulties in trying to do so, he turned to Executive VP Vernon Geddy. He explained that although he had a kitchen staff and prospective manager lined up, it was almost impossible to recruit a serving staff. Without waiters, of course, the restaurant could not open.

A few days later, during a bridge game involving the Geddys and Pomfrets — Geddy said it was around Thanksgiving — W&M President Pomfret mentioned some of the difficulties he had encountered with the War Work Program. Geddy told me that Jack — Pomfret's nickname — "wasn't making a request for help. We were just talking about labor problems on the Peninsula in general and he mentioned the difficulties the college was having in its efforts to find better jobs for the War Work boys employed at Naval Mine Depot.

"That reminded me of John Green's need for waiters, so I suggested that he tell Sharvey Umbeck, who was running the War Work Program, to get in touch with Green and see if something could be worked out to employ young men from the college as waiters."

It was a case where the CW hand fitted perfectly into the W&M glove. Just before the beginning of Christmas vacation in 1942, sixteen War Workers were notified they would become waiters when they returned to W&M in January for their second semester. I was one of the lucky sixteen.

My introduction to the Travis House is permanently etched in my memory. It was a chilly January evening in 1943. A damp, penetrating drizzle drifted slowly down on us as we hurried along Duke of Gloucester Street from the college. Through the gloom and cold, the dim yellow candles in the Travis House beckoned. At the front door we stopped and, hesitant, climbed the slippery steps to tap timidly on the door. Almost immediately we were welcomed by a young, pretty, round-faced blonde and ushered into an empty dining room.

Thawing in the warmth of the old house and the smile of our hostess, we greeted others who had preceded us. As more of our classmates arrived, we became less ill at ease and a few tentative quips broke the ice. Sallies began to fly thick and fast; irrepressible laughter filled the room. Phil Radding — a few years later he added M.D. to his name — performed a burlesque of a French waiter, complete with garbled phrases of pseudo-French. The rest of us doubled with laughter, but at the same time I wondered how a waiter was really supposed to act. Noisy, boisterous and unkempt, we looked like anything but neat, efficient, courteous waiters. And waiters we had to become or we wouldn't be able to remain in school.

The task of converting the Mine Depot laborers into waiters was the responsibility of the Travis House manager, Elizabeth Reynolds. The pretty blonde who had greeted us was her niece, Ruth Lail. Both had come to Williamsburg from homes in Cynthiana, Kentucky.

In later years, Mrs. Reynolds recalled entering the room while Phil Radding was imitating a French waiter and said she didn't know whether to laugh, applaud or chastise him and his audience. She was equally baffled when just before opening the doors for business a couple of weeks later, two of the waiters tied napkins around their waists and performed a hula dance in the entry hall. She wasn't quite so astonished when another youth, breathing heavily, sidled up to her niece and did an imitation of movie actor Charles Boyer. She let him know he was out of bounds, for many of the young men, most of them only a few years younger than the pretty hostess, had crushes on Miss Lail. Her aunt frequently had to shoo amorous young waiters away from her.

Mrs. Reynolds herself often contributed to the lighthearted atmosphere that underlay work at the Travis House. One time, leaning into the dumbwaiter to call instructions down to the kitchen, Mrs. Reynolds inadvertently sent her false teeth down the shaft with her message.

According to Ruth, if her aunt treated the high-spirited William and Mary freshmen as if they were children, it was due to her fear that any missteps on their part would reflect poorly on her and the reputation General Manager John Green wanted Travis House to achieve. "Besides," Ruth added, "Aunt Liddy never raised any boys of her own. The college boys scared her."

Of course Mrs. Reynolds and her niece succeeded in making waiters of the irreverent young men assigned to the Travis House, and in the process we students learned how to earn enough money to climb out of debt.

The youthful waiters also impressed Vernon Geddy and other ranking Restoration officers, for the Travis House became a favorite place for them to entertain guests, either socially or for business purposes. And the boys from William and Mary served many celebrities during the war years, among them Gary Cooper, Henry Fonda, Jeanette MacDonald, Tom Dewey, Kay Kyser and Walter Chrysler.

W&M Alumni Gazette

Sixteen W&M freshmen were its waiters when the Travis House opened for business February 1, 1943. Thirteen of them returned in 1993 for its 50th anniversary, meeting with CW President Robert Wilburn (left) *and W&M President Tim Sullivan* (right). *They were* (from left, front) *the author, then Calvin Tiller, Dr. Philip Radding, Willis Dickerson, Robert Goebel, James Dobyns, Jr., and David Walker.* (Rear) *Everett Baker, Owen Elliott, Ronnie Morton, Robert Porter, Theodore Horner and Robert Whitman.*

One night Mrs. Reynolds reserved one of the three Travis House dining rooms for very special guests. Red Farley and I were assigned to serve them: John D. Rockefeller, Jr.; his wife, Abby Aldrich Rockefeller; and their children: John D. 3rd, Nelson, Laurence, Winthrop and David, plus daughter, Abby.

For anyone who ever worked or dined at Travis House, one memory lingers above all else: scalloped oysters. This succulent dish was provided free as an accompaniment to every entrée. (The waiters consumed more than their fair share, for casseroles of scalloped oysters were always available in the pantry.)

Scalloped oysters were produced by a large, formidable chef remembered as 'Miss Sue', who ran the basement kitchen with an iron hand and a steel meat cleaver, which she waved in menacing fashion when provoked. Nearly every Williamsburg matron or would-be cookbook author — plus an occasional oyster lover — braved Miss Sue's domain seeking her recipe for scalloped oysters. Sue always obliged them. Unfortunately for posterity, the recipes she gave out may have made almost anything else, but they didn't make Travis House scalloped oysters. As I found out later, Miss Sue, like other chefs and popular cooks of the era, believed in keeping trade secrets. Although many cookbooks claim to offer a recipe for 'Travis House Oysters', don't you believe it.

The Travis House reopened for business February 1, 1943, with a staff of William and Mary freshmen as waiters. The arrangement continued until the Travis House closed forever February 28, 1951. During those eight years, 85 young men earned all or part of their undergraduate expenses working there. Upon its closing, the Travis House staff moved en masse to the Kings Arms Tavern, a much larger, purpose-built colonial restaurant. The college continued to provide waiters at the new location until 1992, when the advent of a union ended the arrangement.

Soon after its closing, CW picked up the Travis House and moved it away. Ultimately it was returned to its original 1700s location at the northeast corner of the intersection of Francis and South Henry Streets. Although it is now used as an office by CW, traces of its life as a restaurant are still evident in its interior.

Its former site on Duke of Gloucester Street is now occupied by the reconstructed — and authentic — John Greenhow House. Unlike the Travis House, it's a perfect fit for the 1700s foundations.

'Twas the Night Before Christmas

Here's the second part of Jack Hundley's poem. Again, he pretty much hit the truth:

> Old Williamsburg, it hurts me
> To see you torn up so,

Sometimes I stop and wonder
If they really know
Exactly what it's all about,
Or what they're going to do.
I'll admit it, dear old pal,
'Tis pretty hard on you.
I hate to see your streets torn up,
Your buildings rent apart,
Is it right with you, old pal,
Or does it break your heart?

Although much of the work of restoring Williamsburg remained to be done after World War II, enough had been completed between 1928 and 1942 to transform the town. Those who lived through those 14 years remember vividly the constant disruption. Homes were moved around like pieces on a checkerboard. A huge ditch was dug across Duke of Gloucester Street and parts of Market Square for the Colonial Parkway tunnel. Hotels were built. The population grew, tourists began to arrive and traffic increased.

In those few years, the old business section of town centered around Market Square was wiped out and housed in a brand-new town center in the first block of Duke of Gloucester Street, which began living up — at least in appearance — to the designation given it by President Franklin D. Roosevelt during his 1934 visit. He described it "the most historic avenue in America."

During the wartime years, when little restoration work was carried on, Mr. and Mrs. Rockefeller funded visits to Williamsburg by groups of soldiers, sailors and marines from the armed forces establishments that abounded in Hampton Roads. CW turned the Inn into apartments for families of Army and Navy officers.

Medically discharged from the Navy, I returned to W&M early in 1944 and discovered a town and campus that provided a near dreamlike existence. Coed enrollment had been increased to about one thousand. There were at most two hundred male students but, according to my roommate, also medically discharged, only seventeen were over seventeen years old. Compounding the problem for date-starved coeds, the only other men on campus were officers — mostly married — in the Navy Chaplains School, which had taken over Old Dominion Hall.

My roommate and I were able to pay for tuition, books, food and clothing — even dates — because the town had become loaded with opportunities to earn money. My roommate worked in the campus dining hall, played trombone in the college dance band and made a small fortune as agent for a laundry and dry cleaning firm. I returned to the Travis House and because I was the only waiter over 21, was made wine steward. (During summers I also worked as lifeguard at the Inn swimming pool and at Christmas had a part-time job in the post office.)

In spite of — or maybe because of — jobs and classes, I began to notice a pretty local girl. At first, I'd see her around the Taliaferro-Cole house as I walked to work at the Travis House. Later, when working at the Inn pool, I saw more of her. In those days, local families obtained memberships which permitted them to use the pool, the only one in town. A number of teenage girls were regular patrons, including the one I'd begun to notice. As soon as possible I learned the young lady's name. Her identity brought on an attack of insecurity, for she was Caroline Geddy, Vernon Geddy's daughter.

I learned that my being acquainted with her father didn't qualify me for any special treatment from her, because in those days girls from good families did not become familiar with young men to whom they had not been formally introduced. Although they smiled and exchanged greetings with W&M boys like me, they were very reserved. If I wanted to know her better, I needed an introduction — and had no idea how to get one.

My family had moved to California, too far away to visit, so I lived on campus all year. This meant I was always available for my Travis House job, even during college breaks. For this reason, I was in town Christmas Eve 1945.

At about five in the evening, I left my room in Taliaferro Hall to walk down Duke of Gloucester Street to the Travis House. As I crossed College Corner, I encountered President John Pomfret. W&M's enrollment was so small that he knew most students, so I wasn't surprised to be greeted by name.

He seemed shocked to see me. "Fred! What on earth are you doing here on Christmas Eve?"

I respectfully reminded him that Travis House didn't close its doors on holidays, that some of the waiters had to stay in town to keep it open.

"My goodness!" he said. "I should have thought of that, but I completely forgot. Are many of you working there tonight?"

I told him there were eight of us.

He asked, "And after work do you have plans?"

I told him I supposed we'd go back to the dorm. I didn't add that we had some liquid Christmas awaiting us.

The president stood thoughtfully for a few moments, then asked what time we'd finish work. I told him the doors closed at nine, that we'd probably be finished up by 9:30.

He came to a decision. "Well, we simply can't have you going back to your dormitory rooms on Christmas Eve. After work, you get all the boys together and bring them to my home. Mrs. Pomfret and I will see to it that you have a Christmas Eve party."

It wasn't easy to convince the other guys I wasn't joking. After all, going to the President's House was a big deal. It was only when I agreed to be the one who knocked on the door that they said they'd go along with me.

As it happened, we had a slow night. All the customers were gone by nine o'clock. The result was that I knocked on the President's House door at about ten past nine. Sarah Pomfret opened the door.

For a moment she was obviously shaken. "Oh, dear! You're early." Then she pulled herself together, smiled graciously and told us, "But never mind. We're glad you're here. Come on in."

We had no way of knowing that the Pomfrets were entertaining very good friends for dinner — and that they hadn't quite finished the meal when we showed up. Mrs. Pomfret took all eight of us into the dining room and introduced us to Mr. and Mrs. Vernon Geddy and their daughter, Caroline.

Having been officially introduced to her meant that when I saw Caroline in Rexall's two days later, I was able to ask if she'd like to go to the movies with me. For some incredible reason she agreed. Caroline was a 16-year-old high school senior. I was a 23-year-old college senior. I don't think her mother ever forgave me — but we began dating and were still together when Caroline died fifty years later.

The Pomfrets' Christmas Eve party was a great success, even for the boys who weren't lucky enough to get a date with Caroline. In retrospect, I think that what Jack and Sarah Pomfret did for us that night was symbolic of the way students were treated in those days by Williamsburg people.

Caroline Geddy Frechette and her daughters, Caroline Cole (Cecy) (left) *and Martha Geddy.*

Chapter Four

A Crow Named Jim

In 1942 I arrived in a segregated South. It seems ridiculous now to recall that public places like railroad waiting rooms had four rest rooms, that black folks had to sit at the rear of a bus and that they couldn't even drink from water fountains used by white folks. It took a while for all this to sink in. In the meantime, I laughed with everyone else at the ornate flagpole and brickwork located at the intersection of Jamestown Road and South Boundary Street. A prominent plaque advised one and all that this edifice had been given to the college by the Klu Klux Klan. (At some point in the mid 1900s, it disappeared — not just the plaque, the whole thing.)

When I began working for Colonial Williamsburg, the reality of Jim Crow came home to me. Having achieved the exalted title of Front Office Manager — an honor granted in lieu of a raise, I think — I substituted for the four regular desk clerks of the Inn and Lodge on their days off and performed other duties, like occasionally, replacing the golf pro or becoming a recruiter of blacks for casual labor.

It worked like this: If either the Inn or Lodge was short of help for their most menial positions and I was not otherwise assigned, I'd be provided with a company car — an olive green four-door Chevy — and sent to the corner of Jefferson Avenue and 25th Street in Newport News. That was the unofficial labor market for black guys on the Peninsula. All I had to do was park in front of the assembled labor pool, which varied in size according to the weather. Fair weather would see upwards of fifty black men. Cold or rainy weather reduced the number to a handful of the most desperate. I'd simply roll down the car window and announce that I needed five dishwashers, housemen or yardmen, whatever the hotels required. I'd guarantee them one day's pay and a ride back to Newport News. If they were willing to work more than a day, I told them they'd be provided accommodations in the Franklin House, a dormitory for casual black employees in the Restoration maintenance area. I don't recall ever failing to enlist four or five men.

This was an unpleasant aspect of my job, but my other associations with black employees of the Inn and Lodge were a revelation and often tremendously satisfying. One of the best was the relationship I developed with Nathaniel Reid. From my first days on the desk at the Inn, I was impressed by this bright-eyed, always cheerful bellman (we didn't call them bellboys). He stood out among seven or eight others. Nat was so smart, cooperative and reliable that when the bell captain's job became available, I urged the manager to promote Nat. I'll never know if I had much influence upon his choice, but Nat became the Inn's bell captain. Nat, bless his heart, has always given me credit for his promotion. That's been a source of satisfaction to me.

I used Nat in ways the manager never would have approved. For instance, if I had to go down to the men's room and the manager wasn't around to relieve me, I'd ask Nat to get behind the desk and cover for me. It never occurred to me to lock the cash drawer, because I knew I could trust him and that he'd handle anything that came up efficiently and with aplomb. Fact was, I was so impressed with Nat that I spoke to Vernon Geddy while he was CW's executive vice president. I asked if there wasn't some kind of better, more responsible job in the Restoration for a man as valuable as Nat. I'll never forget Geddy's response, for it was one of the few times I ever saw any trace of shame in his face. "The way things are," he told me, "there's nothing like that we can do for Nat."

A few years later, when Jim Crow was sent packing, Nat received long overdue recognition. Thus, when he retired after a career with the Restoration, Nat was director of service for CW's Division of Visitor Accommodations, a white-collar position.

I worked with interesting black characters at both the Inn and Lodge. The Inn had one with a most unusual name: Thessalonians Judkins. Good-natured and a willing worker, 'Thess' was the Inn's room service waiter. He was so good at his job that CW President Kenneth Chorley allowed no one else to serve him.

When Thess had time off, his substitute was a part-time waiter named Howard (I'm deliberately withholding his last name). I was always

Sixty years after they worked together at the Williamsburg Inn: Nathaniel Reid with the author.

curious about Howard's skin color, which was almost as white as mine — actually whiter in summer when I got a tan. Years after I left the Inn & Lodge, I became friends with his son, Howard Jr., who was also very light skinned. When I got to know him well enough, I asked him about the source of his skin coloration. He told me that his grandmother had been a housemaid for a well-known white couple. The man of that house, a Duke of Gloucester Street merchant, made her pregnant.

When I asked if his white grandfather ever acknowledged the connection, Howard Jr.'s reply was a simple "No". Not only did the white man deny responsibility, he never offered a penny of financial support to either the mother or child. Although I knew the man and had had business dealings with him, I avoided him from then on. His behavior was a sad commentary on the worst aspect of race relations. I could only hope it was not a frequent occurrence.

The Williamsburg Lodge, located just across South England Street from the Inn and Craft House, offered lower prices than the Inn's $10 single and $14 double. As I recall, Lodge rooms rented for $5 or $6 single and $7 or $8 double, so it drew, in addition to tourists, a number of businessmen and salesmen.

Cue Willis was the affable black bell captain at the Lodge. It was impossible not to like the man, even though in retrospect I suspect that Cue may have had some scams going with his merry, cooperative crew of bellmen. I think they provided illegal women and beverages to Lodge guests upon request. It was easy enough to do; access to most of the Lodge guest rooms was not through the lobby. I never caught any of them at it — nor did I try to, for in their day-to-day responsibilities they never let me down.

Immediately behind the Lodge front desk was a room designed for luggage storage. In actual practice, it was the bellmen's hangout. There, out of sight, they conducted a mysterious card game which seemed to have a life of its own, for it never ended. Cue tried to explain it to me, but its rules baffled me. When I was on the Lodge desk, I didn't mind that card game. I knew where I could always find a bellman if I needed one.

I can't recall my days on the desk of the Williamsburg Lodge without warm recollections of some of the folks with whom I worked. My immediate boss was Manager Tommy Moyles, who later managed the Inn. One of the regular room clerks — successor to Moyles — was lanky Bill Batchelder, a man with biting humor and the most indecipherable handwriting of anyone I ever knew. The telephone operator on many of my shifts was a lady named Hattie Lee, who let me know in no uncertain terms that there's a place in western Virginia named Grundy, which was her hometown. Then there were James Wallace and Cornelius Palmer, who spent careers in the Lodge dining room, utterly dependable and always cheerful.

In the first couple of years I worked at the Inn and Lodge there was no information and reception center for visitors to Williamsburg. But tourists with questions swarmed to the front desks of our hotels, particularly the Lodge. This aspect of my duties taught me that I was not endowed by nature with much tolerance for dealing with the public and/or stupid questions — a failing that ultimately drove me from the hotel business.

Colonial Williamsburg took pity on the room clerks in 1949 and built a temporary visitors' reception and information center opposite the Lodge on South England Street — and in the process violated Virginia law. Although at that time the state required separate restrooms for white and colored, CW probably realized that Mr. Rockefeller would never agree to that, so they installed only one for men and one for women. If any state or local officials ever noticed the lack of 'white' and 'colored' signs, they decided to look the other way. CW was never hauled to court.

The Restoration can also take credit for something else it sneaked past both state law and social custom: Fred Epps, Jr., told me the Lodge fed integrated tour groups in private as early as the 1940s. I never personally registered a black guest at either the Inn or the Lodge, but Tommy Moyles told me that the Lodge had done so on a number of occasions.

The Restoration did not, at least in my experience, discriminate against black businesses. Charlie Gary was, to me, evidence of this. Although he had to compete with a couple of white-owned dry cleaners in town, he won all the valet business from both the Inn and Lodge. At the height of his success he had ten employees and built himself a beautiful home in James City County.

While writing this book I had lunch with Nat Reid. It didn't take us long to figure out we were probably the only two people still alive who worked at the Inn during the 1940s. Then we turned to more pleasant topics. Nat summed up the impact of the Restoration on the black population of Williamsburg. He believes that almost all of them went to work for CW during the 1930s in one capacity or another. He said most had at least part of a high school education, but with steady income from their Restoration jobs, they made sure that their children did better.

The result is that Williamsburg's black families, profiting from the steady jobs generated by Mr. Rockefeller's generosity — and believing strongly in the benefits of education — produced a phenomenal number of children who went to college. Many earned advanced degrees and entered professions. Nat Reid's children provide a splendid example. He and his wife, Mary Elizabeth, saw all three of their children through college, and all entered professional occupations. One, Carolyn Reid-Wallace, served as senior vice president for the Public Broadcasting System, then became president of Fisk University.

Camelot, VA 23185

This was Jack Hundley's way of summing up the restoration of Williamsburg:

> To see your homes again restored,
> Your streets and greens well kept,
> I shudder when I think about
> The years that you have slept.
> Your golden opportunity
> Has come to you at last,
> And now you'll take your place again
> As in the glorious past.

He could not have realized that the town had reached its pinnacle, a veritable Camelot for those of us lucky enough to live there. By the middle 1900s, the restoration and reconstruction of buildings in the historic area were virtually complete. Thanks to Mr. Rockefeller's millions, Williamsburg had become a town of unique beauty.

We had this marvelous town pretty much to ourselves. Although the number of visitors increased each year, their presence had not become disruptive, nor had the influx of new residents twisted our community out of shape. Actually, I think most of us were flattered to realize that so many people wanted either to visit or live in Williamsburg.

What kind of town did we live in during the 1950s? To begin with, we knew exactly where it was: the first block of Duke of Gloucester Street, sometimes referred to as 'The Business Block' (we didn't call it 'Merchants Square' in those days — that's a promotional label coined many years later). To us, this was Williamsburg, the town center, the place to meet friends and neighbors, the source of almost all the goods and services we needed for everyday living.

We'd park at the curb on Duke of Gloucester Street or, if no street spaces were open, circle around to one of the parking lots behind the buildings. I can't recall a time when those lots were full. Then, without leaving the first block, we could run whatever errands brought us into town: go to the bank, check our post office box, buy groceries, restock our liquor supply, obtain prescriptions, visit the hardware store, get a hair cut or permanent, eat a meal, go to the movies, gas up the car, arrange for fire insurance, buy clothes, see a lawyer, have a tooth pulled, order flowers, board a Greyhound bus, take home a cake or hang out at the firehouse.

Close by were such businesses as the West End Market at the corner of Prince George and Boundary and, next door to it, Binns Fashions. Scattered around town were a handful of garages, filling stations and automobile dealers. The most important of the functions not in the first block was the city/county courthouse, located on South England Street where the Lodge now has a parking lot. In the late 1940s and the 1950s that courthouse was more than just a place for trying cases.

Historic Duke of Gloucester Street before cars were prohibited.

Newport News Daily Press

Anonymous

Business block in front of Five &Ten, a typical 1950s Saturday.

It housed meetings of both the Williamsburg City Council and James City County Board of Supervisors. We paid our taxes and voted there, too. And after finishing our business at the courthouse, we could walk over to the Lodge Coffee Shop to meet friends and sip the best coffee in town for five cents a cup.

That South England Street courthouse was torn down, of course, and succeeded by others (I've lost count). The most recent is located in what's known as New Town. Maybe it will remain for a while.

The most overwhelming concentration of businesses was in the first block of Duke of Gloucester. A trip there was like a casual talk over the fence with a multitude of neighbors. Indeed, if we saw people we didn't know, we assumed they were tourists — and were probably correct.

The business block wasn't only for white people. Particularly on Saturdays, scores of black folks congregated on the spacious sidewalks around the state liquor store (Virginia was a dry state in those days), not only to patronize the store, but to meet friends and neighbors.

We were probably most familiar with Curly Atkinson at the grocery store, Steve Sacalis at his College Corner restaurant — with Ham Smith out front, leaning on a fender of his police car — and the Watson brothers at the hardware store, Bob Duncan at the bank or Albert Douglas at the bakery. There was a closeness among us, a sense of belonging. Perhaps the best example of this feeling took place every weekday morning at the Rexall Pharmacy.

Just off the post office arcade — the interior corridor linking Duke of Gloucester with the post office — the drugstore maintained a small soda fountain. There were no stools there, but a few booths lined the glass windows along the arcade for those who wished to consume shakes, sodas and sandwiches. The soda fountain was the centerpiece, however. That was the morning meeting place and forum for most of the town's business, professional and political leaders. It was where one learned what was going on in Williamsburg.

Business block, the line at the ABC store on a typical 1950s Saturday.

Anonymous

Shortly after 10 a.m., we'd order our five-cent cups of coffee — except for Mayor Polly Stryker. When they saw him crossing Duke of Gloucester on his way to the pharmacy, the women behind the counter made sure a nickel Coke — no ice — awaited him in the usual wasp-waisted glass.

Accompanying our drinks, each of us received a five-cent cash register printout. We called them chits. The pharmacy issued them for us to give to the cashier with our money when we left. Those chits became part of a game. Each new arrival, upon receiving his coffee, had to match coins with the holder of all the previously issued chits. If he lost, he inherited all the chits. Thus on most mornings, our coffee was free, but on an unlucky day we'd wind up buying coffee for everyone. That could cost as much as a dollar and a half.

Not everyone showed up for morning coffee every day, of course, but even a short list of regulars is a "Who's Who" of 1950s Williamsburg. To name just a few, I recall, besides Mayor Stryker, men like Russ Carneal (then a member of the House of Delegates and later a Circuit Court

Anonymous

Williamsburg Jaycees, spring 1950.
(From left, seated): *Chester Baker, Russ Carneal, Don Taylor, Hank Strong.*
(Standing): *Al Haak, David Hendeson, author, Bob Sager, Horace "Hunky" Henderson.*

Anonymous

Young Women's Club Dance 1951, Williamsburg Lodge Ballroom. (From left) *Chester & Helen Baker, Tommy & Micou Savage, unidentified couple, Howard & Betty Smith.*

judge), Jimmy Vaiden (chairman of the James City County Board of Supervisors), Realtor G.T. Brooks, CW vice president Duncan Cocke, phone company manager Tom Cutler, postmaster Merritt Foster, lawyer Channing Hall Jr., revenue commissioner Billy Morecock and oil dealer Bill Schreiber.

It's almost impossible to convey the sense of camaraderie that existed among those who met for morning coffee at Rexall's. Although completely informal, it was very exclusive. Visitors and strangers were not welcome and there were unwritten, undeclared criteria for acceptance. A sense of humor was chief among them, for stinging repartee was the norm and any sign of pretentiousness was the cause for instant, overwhelming derision.

This is not to say that all those wonderful Williamsburg men — and their women — were without faults and flaws. Certainly, they were much like the residents of other small Southern towns in exhibiting many of the gentle, courteous qualities that carried over from the late 1800s. They were wonderful neighbors and were ever willing to help those in need. By and large, the menfolk tipped their hats to and opened doors for ladies. They believed in honor, were loyal to their friends and cheered lustily when a band played "Dixie". They tended to be conservative Democrats — Republican was a dirty word — shot ducks and other game by the thousand, and did not readily accept newcomers.

They also consumed large amounts of whiskey. Williamsburg was a party town, with an event almost every evening. As a young married couple, Caroline and I attended many of them. Fortunately, we couldn't keep up with the drinking that went on. There was no wine, no beer. The liquid of the day was basic bourbon.

That's where I learned the meaning of 'bourbon and branch' — a shot of whiskey with a few drops of water. It may not have been immediately lethal, but its long-term effects are evident in the life spans chiseled in the granite of Cedar Grove's stones.

Name Dropping

Shirley Temple showed up in April 1938 at the height of her popularity and celebrated her tenth birthday with daughters of CW officials. Her next visit was in 1976 when, as U.S. chief of protocol, she came with the president of Finland. Although Shirley's return was a matter of note, the visit of a foreign president was not of earth-shaking

Courtesy of Joan Green Apter

Shirley Temple's 10th Birthday Party, Williamsburg Inn, April 23, 1938. (From left) *Suzanne Green, Caroline Geddy, Shirley Temple, Lois Kendrew.* (Foreground) *Joan Green.*

Newport News Daily Press

Thirty-eight years later, Shirley returned to Williamsburg as U.S. chief of protocol with Urho Kekkonen, president of Finland.

importance to us. Visits to Williamsburg by presidents and other leaders of nations have been, if not a dime a dozen, at least quite frequent.

Harding, Coolidge and Roosevelt visited in the years before World War II. Apparently Kennedy ignored us, but all other U.S. presidents since the war have visited. The town also hosted Winston Churchill, Queen Mother Elizabeth and Prince Charles. Other visitors included the president of Romania, the king and queen of Greece, King Hussein of Jordan, Emperor Hirohito and Prince Akihito from Japan, and U.S. VIPs like John Foster Dulles. Entertainers and actors used Williamsburg as a stage. Dave Garroway conducted his TV show at the Inn. John Wayne and Perry Como staged a TV Christmas show at the Governor's Palace. Cary Grant acted in movie scenes filmed in town. There were many others, including those who simply came for an unofficial visit or for dinner, like the celebrities served at the Travis House by W&M students.

Perhaps some of us became a bit blasé about our exposure to big-name visitors, but not Sam Peach. Sam belonged to a family of law officers. Two or three of his brothers served in the Newport News Police

James E. Mays

Ike Visits Our Town.
(From left) *President Eisenhower, CW chairman (and Arkansas governor) Winthrop Rockefeller, secret service agent, author.*

Department. Sam himself was a deputy sheriff in Warwick County before he lost a leg in an accident. His many friends convinced Vernon Geddy that Sam could handle a job as security officer for the Restoration. "One of the smartest moves I ever made," Geddy said. He described an incident that made Sam Peach a Williamsburg legend.

One day, a mentally unbalanced man waving a pistol entered the CW offices, rounded up a group of employees — including Geddy — and threatened to shoot them. Sam Peach came rushing from his office on his wooden leg, took in the situation, then limped up to the gunman. "Sam told him to give him the danged gun or he'd kick his butt," Geddy said. "Darn if the man didn't meekly hand his gun to Sam!"

During Peach's tenure it was part of his job to help protect famous visitors, so he was almost always physically close to them, particularly if they left their vehicles to walk to locations in the historic area. Watching him hobble gamely along nearby often prompted English-speaking VIPs to engage Sam in conversation, which thoroughly delighted the former deputy sheriff.

As he put it, "Where in the world 'cept here in Williamsburg would a poor ol' country boy like me get a chance to meet all these famous people?"

But Sam, like most Williamsburg people who knew them, considered members of the Rockefeller family as the best of all — and not because of the money John D. Jr. gave to the Restoration. It was because of the unpretentious humility and thoughtfulness they consistently displayed.

Although I served the Rockefellers when they dined at the Travis House in the spring of 1943, my adrenaline was probably working at a high pitch. I was so anxious to do everything properly, I hardly had time to look at the individuals. Thus the only two family members I remembered accurately were Father and Mother — John D. Jr. and Abby. Their sons and daughter didn't really register in my memory.

Six years later, when I came on duty at the Inn desk one afternoon in 1949, the clerk I relieved advised me that John D. 3rd was in Room 213 — the Inn's finest. At the time, he was chairman of the Colonial Williamsburg board of directors, but for the life of me, I couldn't remember exactly what he looked like. Late in the evening a tall, pleasant-faced man came to the desk. He looked vaguely familiar.

"I wonder," he said very diffidently, "if you happen to have a pair of pliers or a small wrench I could borrow?"

I told him we had no tools at the desk, but was there a problem in his room? We had people available to fix things.

"Oh, I don't want to bother anyone," he said. "It's just a small thing."

"What kind of thing?"

"Really nothing, just a drip in the shower. Nothing to bother with."

He started to leave.

"But sir!" I said, "We have maintenance men just sitting around waiting for things to do." Which was a slight exaggeration, but seemed appropriate. "Let me send one of them up to fix it."

"Well, all right, as long as it's not too much trouble."

"What room are you in, sir?"

"Two thirteen." His identity was no longer vague.

That was typical of the self-effacing Rockefellers. John D. 3rd served as chairman of the board until 1953, when he was succeeded by his brother Winthrop, governor of Arkansas. Many Williamsburgers are of the opinion that Winthrop was more devoted to Williamsburg than any of his siblings. In spite of his gubernatorial duties, he spent a lot of time in the 'Burg and, I'm told, never neglected his CW responsibilities.

Actually, my first contact with a Rockefeller was just that: physical contact. As a freshman, I didn't know that John D. Jr. and Abby occasionally went to a movie at the Williamsburg Theater and always sat in aisle seats in the back row. One spring evening in 1943, before I had served the Rockefeller family at the Travis House, I decided to catch the late show.

I wanted my usual aisle seat in the back row, but the first two seats were occupied by an old couple, so I made an appropriate excuse and waited in the darkness for the man and woman to stand and allow me to pass to a seat beyond them. In the process I accidentally stepped on the man's foot. He uttered an "Ouch", I muttered an apology, and squeezed beyond them to an empty seat. I thought no more about it until after the show when the usher, classmate Harmon Hoffman, caught me in the lobby.

"You know whose toe you stepped on?" he laughed. "Mr. Rockefeller's!"

For many years after giving the Restoration its start, Mr. Rockefeller spent several weeks each spring and autumn at Bassett Hall, his Williamsburg residence.

He usually took a walk in the afternoon but had no habitual pattern. He might be seen anywhere in the historic area — if you knew what to look for, that is. He melted into the crowds of tourists, looking like an elderly visitor enjoying the sights. That was about as anonymous and unnoticeable as anyone could be in Williamsburg.

The praiseworthy aspect of his walks was that even if local folks happened to recognize him, they respected his privacy. Although they'd say "hello", I never heard of anyone attempting to ask for his autograph or otherwise interrupt his walk.

One late spring afternoon, while driving down Duke of Gloucester Street with a thunderstorm threatening a downpour at any moment, I saw Mr. Rockefeller walking toward Bassett Hall as fast as he could. I pulled over and called for him to hop in my car before the rain began. He did so. Moments later, the deluge struck. When I delivered him to the front door of his home at Bassett Hall, he very kindly invited me in, but I had to decline.

It was through Caroline — and she through her father — that I enjoyed a privilege not granted to many young men. Like almost everyone else who knew him, Mr. Rockefeller was captivated by Vernon Geddy. They became fast friends. The Rockefeller wedding gift to Caroline was by far the most exquisite she received and later, when Mr. Rockefeller learned that Caroline and I planned to visit New York, he insisted that we call upon him.

While in New York we took an elevator to the 56th floor of Rockefeller Center and were swept into Mr. Rockefeller's presence by staff members who had obviously been prompted to expect us. He was not a large man, so behind a large desk in a big, dark-hued room, he seemed even smaller than he actually was. He rose from behind the desk to greet us.

We did not have an extended conversation, but Mr. Rockefeller wanted to know how long we'd be in New York and what we planned to do during our visit. Caroline told him we'd stay about a week and hadn't really made any plans except to see the sights and, if possible, a Broadway show.

When we left Rockefeller Center, we walked around midtown for a couple of hours, then returned to our hotel. As we entered the lobby, a room clerk called out. He had a large envelope for us containing tickets to several shows, among them *Call Me Madam* with Ethel Merman, *Bell, Book and Candle* with Rex Harrison and *Lend An Ear*, Carol Channing's first Broadway appearance. A note accompanying the tickets read, as I recall, 'Mr. Rockefeller hopes you will enjoy these.'

Believe me, we did.

Colonial Williamsburg Foundation

Winston Churchill, escorted by CW President Kenneth Chorley.

The Tiger and the Pussycat

Kenneth Chorley was CW president from 1935 to 1958. If he had a dominating characteristic, it was his intense and devoted loyalty to Mr. Rockefeller. It made for a strange combination, for Chorley was a very large man. In a physical sense, I think he was twice the size of his boss. And unlike the gentle millionaire, he terrorized many of the people who worked for him.

Son of a clergyman, Chorley left home while in his teens, forgoing a college education for jobs as a laborer in railroad construction. Considering his size, the strength he must have developed wielding a pick and shovel or sledgehammer probably made it possible for him to hold his own in the rough world of railroad building. At some point, Chorley must have been employed in Standard Oil operations, for the story told around Williamsburg is that he came to the oil company's attention because of his success as a strikebreaker. This apparently began his career as a troubleshooter for Rockefeller interests. Along the way Chorley entered the employ of John D. Jr.

Vernon Geddy intimated — he never came right out and said it — that in the early or mid-1930s Mr. Rockefeller became dissatisfied with the progress of the restoration of Williamsburg. In almost the same breath, Geddy would describe CW's first president, Colonel Arthur Woods, as a nice guy. Too nice, perhaps. Troubleshooter Chorley replaced him as CW's president in 1935.

There's no question that Chorley terrorized many of the top people in the Goodwin Building, then CW's headquarters. He combined his large, powerful body with what could be a fierce, intimidating manner. Even when he wasn't angry, he seemed to be, which did not endear him to those who were timid. On the other hand, KC — as he was known — tended to respect those who weren't intimidated.

Geddy, who was his Number Two man, dealt with Chorley on a daily basis. "He's a pussycat," he grinned, "but if you act like you're scared of him, he'll chase you out of the office and run you all the way to Toano." He said KC didn't like 'yes men', that a subordinate could say 'no' without losing his job, but KC expected that person to have solid reasons for his dissention.

I witnessed an incident that attested to Chorley's tiger/pussycat personality. I went on duty at the Williamsburg Inn one afternoon with a brand-new telephone operator on duty in the cubicle adjacent to the room rack. I can't recall her name, but I remember she was a pretty red-headed, freckled girl of around twenty. Like all our operators, she wore a headset with a mouthpiece at her chest. Shortly after five o'clock, although I was busy checking in some arrivals, I heard her arguing heatedly with someone on the line, then abruptly yanking the plug from her board.

She asked me, "Who's the man in the Quarter?"

The Quarter was the name of the cottage in which President Chorley always stayed when in Williamsburg. When I told her, her face paled.

"I think I just lost my job," she said. "He accused me of not giving him an important message he was expecting. I told him I just came on duty at three and didn't know anything about any message for him. He yelled at me and I got mad and told him I wouldn't take that from anyone. Then I pulled the plug."

I feared that she might very well be fired for what she did, but I did my best to console her and assure her I'd back her up.

When Chorley came storming into the lobby and up to the desk a few minutes later, I braced myself to defend the girl, but before I could open my mouth he waved me aside and pointed at her. "Can you handle that switchboard while I speak to that young lady?"

I had no recourse. I took her place at the switchboard as she walked, somewhat unsteadily, to face Chorley, who towered over her, for she was only about five feet tall to his six-four.

His words went something like, "Miss, I apologize for my behavior. I could tell you I've had a rough day and that Aldie Boyer [Chorley's assistant] got my message, but that's no excuse for the way I acted. Please forgive me."

The young telephone operator received a large flower arrangement from KC at her home the next day.

As a reporter for the *Richmond Times-Dispatch* I dealt with Chorley fairly often. I came to like and admire him. He didn't duck tough questions and always gave me straight answers. And one time, when we talked about the death of Vernon Geddy, he shed tears. It takes a strong man to show that kind of emotion.

Colonial Williamsburg Foundation

Vernon Geddy's retirement from CW.
(From left): *Vernon Spratley, Dick Talley, Kenneth Chorley, Ed Alexander* (behind Chorley's shoulder), *Geddy, Bela Norton, John Green, John D. Rockefeller, Jr., Ed Kendrew, Irma Williams. Rockefeller was chairman of CW's Board, Chorley its president. Talley, Alexander, Norton, Green and Kendrew were vice presidents. Spratley, later a circuit court judge in Hampton, was Geddy's assistant and Irma Williams was Geddy's secretary.*

Of one thing I'm certain — from the words and actions of Vernon Geddy and other men and women who worked closely with him, KC was the man most responsible for transforming the Williamsburg dream into reality. If he had a weakness, it may have been in his devotion to Mr. Rockefeller. That kind of utter loyalty could backfire. I witnessed such an incident. I had just relieved the regular Inn room clerk one afternoon when Mr. Rockefeller, as he occasionally did, entered the Inn lobby. After exchanging greetings with me and the bellmen, he stepped outdoors to the patio behind the lobby.

Obviously informed of Mr. Rockefeller's presence, General Manager Green sped from his office and out the back door to join our favorite millionaire. They conversed for a few minutes, then Mr. Rockefeller continued on his walk and Green returned to his office.

About forty-five minutes later, a Restoration flatbed truck and landscaping crew drove into the patio. Before I knew it, they had cut down one of the trees and covered the space with flagstones. When they left an hour later, the patio looked as if the tree had never existed. For a moment I wondered why Mr. Rockefeller had the tree removed, then forgot the matter.

Many years later, after his retirement, I asked Green if he remembered the incident. He did. "My conversation with Junior [the CW term for Mr. Rockefeller] was mostly about the landscaping. At one point, he indicated one of the trees and said something to the effect that it didn't look like the others. It seemed just a casual remark with no significance. When I returned to my office, KC phoned about some business matters. I told him I'd had a talk with Junior and as usual, KC wanted to know everything Junior did and said, so I included his mention of the tree. You know the rest. If Junior took a breath, KC exhaled."

I'm sure that Mr. Rockefeller would have been thoroughly embarrassed to learn that his casual remark could lead to such a drastic action. It made me wonder how often things like that were done in his name without his knowledge.

Chapter Five

Life With A Goose

In 1977, for a slidefilm celebrating the 50th anniversary of the Restoration, I wrote that "living with the Restoration is like living in the nest of the goose that lays golden eggs. Sometimes it gets a bit crowded, and occasionally one of its big, beautiful eggs lands on our heads, but we're not about to kick that goose out of the nest."

I believe this was a fairly accurate assessment of the townspeople's attitude toward Colonial Williamsburg at that time. We knew how strongly Mr. Rockefeller felt about being a good neighbor — before he died we held a community meeting to let him know how much we appreciated both his generosity and his neighborliness — and we felt that those administering CW were conscientiously following his lead.

Carl Humelsine succeeded KC as president of Colonial Williamsburg in 1958. Before that, he served as executive vice president. His home during that period was the Taliaferro-Cole House at the corner of Nassau and Duke of Gloucester Streets. (Taliaferro is pronounced "Tolliver.") During several of those years, Caroline and I lived in the Taliaferro-Cole kitchen, a separate building on Nassau Street behind the Humelsine residence. We became good friends.

Not long after we became neighbors, Carl purchased a sailboat. For its maiden voyage from a Gloucester Point marina, he graciously invited Caroline and me to join his wife, Mary, as his crew. The vessel, as I recall, was eighteen or twenty feet in length, with a mainsail and jib. Steering was performed with a tiller — and only 'Captain' Humelsine was permitted to handle it. Carl took his responsibility as skipper seriously. Upon our boarding the vessel, he informed us that when the captain told us to jump up, we weren't to come down until he gave us permission to do so.

Mary and Caroline had prepared lunch, so after a pleasant sail down the York toward Chesapeake Bay, we lowered the sails, dropped the anchor and enjoyed a picnic. As we ate and enjoyed the weather — it was a beautiful day on Chesapeake Bay — the breeze slowly shifted and increased. This complicated Carl's steering, for now, with little or no experience, he had to sail against the wind to return to Gloucester Point. He knew enough to tack — zig-zag — to do so. He did not, however, know enough about the York River shallows to avoid its hazards.

As we flew along, close-hauled, the centerboard suddenly began to chatter, which meant it was hitting bottom. I hurriedly pulled it up. Without the centerboard, the craft became uncontrollable and slid rapidly downwind. We lowered the sails, but the wind continued to blow us in the wrong direction. Carl raced to the bow and dropped the anchor overboard, but it was unnecessary. We had already run aground.

I took off my shoes and gingerly lowered myself overboard. I needn't have bothered being careful. The water barely covered my ankles. We were in less than a foot of water with a heavy wooden boat that required at least two feet to float. The nearest land was about a half mile away and there was no telling where the water deepened.

We spent most of that gorgeous afternoon pushing, pulling and cursing that sailboat across the flats of the York River until it floated again. Carl was very forgiving when, as the years went by, I persisted in needling him about his maiden voyage, for I'm sure he would have enjoyed drowning me, but he graciously permitted me to survive.

Years later, when Carl and Mary found an attractive getaway home on the Piankatank River above Fishing Bay, Carl acquired a beautiful Dutch-built sailboat. To show us how much his skills had improved, he invited Caroline and me, together with author Burke Davis and his wife, to join him and Mary for a cruise on the vessel. I would have thought he'd keep the boat at Fishing Bay, at the mouth of the Chesapeake, because the Piankatank has a narrow, twisting channel which is not suitable for sailing vessels. But Carl moored his sailboat at the pier in front of his home. When we shoved off, I assumed he'd use his motor to reach the open water of Chesapeake Bay near Gwynn's Island, but he didn't. He raised the sails and adroitly maneuvered his craft down the difficult Piankatank. Then, to show that his piloting had not been a matter of luck, he repeated the feat returning upstream. I never again needled him about running aground.

Another outstanding memory of neighbor Humelsine was of his experience with a dog. About 1955, he acquired a gray Weimaraner named Scholar, who was given the run of an enclosed yard. As dogs go, Scholar was beautiful and friendly — except to the men who came weekly to pick up trash. That's when Scholar took on the character of a pit bull. Unless someone held Scholar on a leash, the trash men couldn't

Carl Humelsine (right) *president of CW from 1958 to 1973, takes a carriage ride on Duke of Gloucester Street with Winthrop Rockefeller, CW board chairman from 1953 to 1973.*

Colonial Williamsburg Foundation

enter the yard. The holder, as often as not, was either Caroline or me — or both of us. Scholar was large and strong.

Carl was very proud of that animal. One day I noticed that Scholar was not around. Carl explained he wanted Scholar's help when he went duck hunting, so he had enrolled Scholar in a hunting dog school in the Shenandoah Valley. The training program was to last about six weeks. For this reason, I was quite surprised to see Scholar back in the Humelsine's yard after only a week.

Carl was reluctant to explain, but I pressed him. With great embarrassment, he admitted that Scholar had flunked out of school.

"Why?" I asked.

"He's afraid of trees."

Scholar disappeared soon afterward. I never asked what happened to him and Carl never explained. He swallowed his disappointment and went on with his life — an attitude that helped him to weather some of the storms he faced during his years as head of CW.

Humelsine may have had problems with Scholar, but there was nothing wrong with his administrative abilities and his loyalty to the marvelous dream of the Reverend W.A.R. Goodwin and John D. Rockefeller, Jr. Although Kenneth Chorley rescued the Restoration and put it on track, KC never had the rapport with people and employees that Carl Humelsine achieved. Both were highly intelligent, honest and open, but in my opinion Humelsine faced tougher problems than KC.

I believe he was the first CW leader to publicly describe the core problem facing Colonial Williamsburg in its efforts to become self-supporting. Very simply, the historic area of Williamsburg is open to everyone, for the streets are public. As long as a visitor obeys traffic laws, he is free to go anywhere within the restored area that is not private property. In a 1972 statement to the press, Humelsine noted that "Last year nearly 40 per cent or approximately 400,000 of our visitors did not purchase tickets or otherwise share in the cost of their visits."

Williamsburg's historic area is, in effect, an outdoor museum without gates. It's also a municipal park. Mingling with tourists on Duke of Gloucester Street — strolling, walking their dogs, jogging or biking — are hundreds of local people, including college students and residents of nearby counties. They've discovered it's a marvelous place to relax or exercise — and it's free.

CW's first solution to this problem, implemented in January 1973, was to require visitors to show general admission tickets to gain access to all sights and services in the historic area such as craft shops, tour buses, films and evening lectures. Local residents would continue to get free annual passes, but only if they asked for them. Duke of Gloucester Street remained open to all, however.

Apparently this change in policy did not solve CW's problems with non-paying visitors. Two years later Humelsine embarked upon a campaign aimed at enclosing the historic area of Williamsburg. He did not elaborate on the methods that would be used to accomplish this, but noted that Yosemite National Park, Jackson Hole and other locations with problems like those facing Williamsburg operated in this fashion. He said there were two main reasons why CW wanted to seal off the area: to increase income and to prevent people from overrunning the 173-acre outdoor museum which the historic area had become.

Humelsine wanted automobile traffic eliminated and suggested closure of Francis Street upon completion of Route 199. This suggestion never won much support and finally died. So did the idea of enclosing the historic area, but for a different reason: When CW acquired tracts of public property in the middle of the city in 1930, it guaranteed 'free access to the public'. The agreement constitutes a use restriction on Palace Green, Market Square Green and several parcels of open space around the Powder Magazine. There was no way to require admission tickets for folks who wanted to visit them.

Despite the difficulties, the city did what it could to help CW, particularly with respect to traffic control, because living with the goose and its golden egg had become uncomfortable during the 1960s, not only for the locals, but for the goose. As more and more tourists arrived, the presence of motor vehicles parked haphazardly in the historic area completely destroyed the colonial atmosphere presented by the restored and reconstructed buildings. Humelsine led a successful CW effort to persuade city council to close Duke of Gloucester Street to motor vehicles.

Denying use of Duke of Gloucester Street to vehicular traffic meant, of course, that locals could no longer use it either. The howls of some outraged citizens were louder than those emanating from Eastern State Hospital patients. None of us really liked the ban, but most agreed it was necessary. And by and large, we could sympathize with CW's problem with non-paying visitors — but saw no practical way to solve it.

Neither could Humelsine as he struggled during his tenure as CW president to solve the problem presented by the openness of the historic area. He felt — not unreasonably — that some means should be found to limit access to the areas maintained at great expense by the Restoration, but he was never able to come up with a workable solution to the problem — nor have any of his successors.

Some of the changes brought about by the growth of the Restoration eroded community support. One of the changes involved the Williamsburg Fire Department. Its totally inadequate firehouse on Henry Street was shut down and the department moved to what was Person's Garage and gas station at the corner of Francis and Boundary Streets, now occupied by Berrett's Restaurant. The old firehouse and farmers' market next to it were obliterated to make room for a post office, which itself was later relocated.

Although it upset many housewives who used the farmers' market, this change made it possible for fire vehicles — many of which were acquired through the efforts of volunteer firemen — to be housed under cover. It was a fitting conclusion to a remarkable turnabout in fire protection which grew out of a partnership between the city and the Restoration.

Thirty Years' Worth of Mayors

Henry Morris Stryker served as mayor of Williamsburg for twenty years. He was known to everyone in town as 'Polly', a nickname derived from his mother's maiden name, Pollard. After watching him preside at city council meetings, I described him to strangers as the world's worst dentist and best small town mayor. I say this with affection, for I believe there's truth in both claims.

Polly was Vernon Geddy's closest friend, so it was natural when I began having trouble with my teeth that I went to Dr. Stryker for treatment. This was not one of my best decisions. I turned to another dentist after one visit.

I asked Geddy why Polly was so casual and unprofessional about dentistry.

"That's because he never wanted to be a dentist," Geddy explained. "But his mother made him go to dental school. He hates his work."

But Polly dearly loved serving on city council — and Williamsburg residents dearly loved Polly, for when they went to the polls, he invariably led the ticket. They obviously didn't give a hoot about his dental credentials.

Heavy and slow-moving, with more of a rustic drawl than Geddy, Polly did not seem to have the makings of a popular public figure, but

South Henry Street fire station in 1955. This photo was used in the Richmond Times-Dispatch *to illustrate how new vehicles acquired by volunteer firemen had outstripped its capacity. Building in background on Francis Street is the Travis House, which was moved there from Duke of Gloucester Street and served as headquarters for Jamestown's 350th anniversary celebration. It was then moved to its present (and original) location on the opposite corner of the intersection. Seasons Arcade now occupies the site of the old firehouse.*

he had a certain charisma — an indefinable trait that caused people to trust him. And though he described himself as 'an old country boy', you'd never have known it to watch him play host to world figures. As Williamsburg grew, Mayor Stryker grew with it.

Polly invariably visited the Geddy home on Holly Hill at dinner time — just in time for dessert. His timing was uncanny. Vernon and Carrie Cole were so used to it that they'd have a chair ready for him at Vernon's elbow and an extra dessert awaiting his arrival. I believe he deserved it, for to Williamsburg he was both main course and dessert as long as he lived.

After dessert. Mayor Polly Stryker, familiar visitor at Holly Hill. Caroline Frechette (left) *and her mother, Carrie Cole Geddy.*

After Vernon Geddy's death, Polly continued his dessert-time visits to the home of Vernon's son, known to everyone in Williamsburg as Bud Geddy. Watching them together at a dinner table, I could not have predicted that between them, they'd serve as mayors for thirty years

Newport News Daily Press

Vernon M. Geddy, Jr., known to all as 'Bud', was a prominent Williamsburg attorney and served as mayor for 10 years.

— Polly for twenty, Bud for ten. On the surface, they were so different that such a suggestion would have seemed the height of folly: Polly, who looked and spoke like a good-natured old country boy, and Bud, quiet, thoughtful and very much a product of Princeton and the University of Virginia Law School. Polly, outgoing, as comfortable as an old shoe; Bud, reserved and private.

What didn't show, of course, was their intense loyalty to Williamsburg, their conscientiousness and their innate common sense. That's probably why they invariably received the most votes when they ran for seats on city council — and why fellow council members consistently chose them as mayor. Both served on CW boards and myriad local committees, commissions and boards. They must have been patient men to have endured all those meetings.

Although Bud's personality was unlike that of his father, his character was very much like that of Geddy Senior. His integrity and sense of honor were so strong that it brought out the best in others. He was, in every important way, a splendid example of a Virginia gentleman.

Flycaster

Fortunately for residents of James City County, the commonwealth's attorney for many years was Robert T. Armistead. Although he was elected by and represented residents of both Williamsburg and James City County, his presence was required only at meetings of the county board of supervisors. I don't think it's an exaggeration to say that Armistead, a Williamsburg resident, was the most influential man in the county during his years as commonwealth's attorney.

He was also an avid outdoorsman. One of his favorite ways of relaxing and getting away from workday pressures was to take a five-minute drive to Tutter's Neck, a private pond in which he had a proprietary interest. One afternoon I was fortunate enough to be invited by Armistead to accompany him to his sylvan hideaway. He carried a fly rod and a small box of flies. We boarded a small boat and paddled quietly along the edge of the pond, my host silently examining the quiet water that lay under overhanging trees.

"This is good," he said. We stopped paddling. He whipped his fly line back and forth a couple of times, then placed a fly on the water in the shade beneath a branch. The water exploded as a large bass struck it. Bob carefully and efficiently worked the fish close to the boat. I had enough sense to grab a net and bring the thrashing bass aboard. I guess it was close to five pounds.

I exclaimed about it as Armistead carefully removed the hook from its mouth and returned the fish to the pond. Luckily, I didn't tell him how lucky he was, because I soon learned that luck had very little to do with his success. Several more times he cast a fly accurately to spots where he believed bass were lurking and not only did he invariably put the fly exactly where he aimed, he often reeled in a fish. It came to me that Armistead worked the same way he fished. He knew his subject thoroughly, knew where the truth lay and had the means and skill to reach it.

Thus, except for the most simple and obvious of matters, the supervisors invariably turned to Armistead for advice. When asked, he gave it. The supervisors listened to him because he knew his subject, dealt with it intelligently and fairly, and played no favorites. As a result, they usually voted as he recommended. It's my opinion that Bob Armistead almost single-handedly kept James City from serious trouble during the years he attended meetings of the board.

Frank Armistead, Bob's father, was the circuit court judge in Williamsburg when I became a reporter. He died in 1952. Four years later, his son was appointed circuit court judge and served until 1977. Local attorneys who tried cases before Judge Robert Armistead were unanimous in praising him as tough and very fair, but with little tolerance for lawyers who had not prepared their cases thoroughly.

Robert T. Armistead

Steve Harris, veteran Williamsburg attorney and former city councilman, said Bob Armistead "took you to task and stopped proceedings if you were not prepared or had not read the code." He added, "He had as good a legal mind as anyone I've come across, a tremendous intellect. He was a well-respected judge and had a very keen sense of justice."

Armistead's legal mind and intellect came into play several times over the years in the running battles he had with Colonial Williamsburg. No need here to detail them, but it's interesting to note that he never lost any of them.

Headlines We Didn't Need

In the space of little more than six years, William and Mary provided Williamsburg with two national news stories we could have done without. The first began innocently enough in the publication office of *The Flat Hat*, our undergraduate weekly, on a Saturday afternoon in early February 1945. That was the day each week we put together an issue of the paper.

Marilyn Kaemmerle, '45, known to us as 'Mac', was editor. From her desk, which was beside mine, she tossed me a typewritten sheet. We invariably traded copies of whatever we wrote for *The Flat Hat* — hers for her editorial, mine for my weekly column — seeking constructive criticism. "What do you think of this?" she asked.

Her proposed editorial was headlined "Lincoln's Job Half Done" and suggested, quite strongly, that although Lincoln had freed the slaves, his job was not finished, for blacks were not yet really free. She cited examples of the ways in which Jim Crow still prevented racial equality in the South.

As soon as I read it, I tossed it back to her. I've never forgotten my advice, "I wouldn't touch this with a ten-foot pole."

Mac, who viewed the world idealistically and courageously, ignored my realistic, cowardly advice. She printed her editorial in the Lincoln's Birthday issue of *The Flat Hat*.

Her editorial created a furor — not just on campus, not just in Williamsburg, not just in Virginia, but nationwide. The W&M board of visitors, the college's governing body, composed mostly of conservative men reared during bitter Reconstruction years, supported by like-minded members of the Virginia General Assembly, demanded Mac's scalp for printing such heresies.

Across America, newspapers and radio broadcasters, fed by wire services, played up the story. When we staged a student strike to support Mac's right to print her opinion, news accounts interpreted our stand as support for her position. That did not diminish headlines and publicity. Editorials and quotations pro and con filled the media. Youths from the area cruised Richmond and Jamestown Roads near the campus pelting male students with beer bottles and yelling crude, obscene remarks at coeds.

There was fear that if the outsiders got their hands on Mac, they might lynch her. Dean of Women Grace Landrum ensured her safety by hiding Mac in her home. In the meantime, the board of visitors demanded that Mac be expelled. To his credit, W&M President Pomfret refused to knuckle under. He couldn't save Mac's job as editor — she was fired on a technicality having nothing to do with the subject of her editorial — but he refused to expel her. Mac was able to graduate in June of 1945 with her class.

Six years later, another tragic, distasteful episode blackened William and Mary's long and illustrious record. During this period, the college's football team had been competing successfully on a national level, but the campus community had for months been hearing rumors of questionable practices in the athletic department. Before long it became obvious something was terribly wrong with the W&M football program.

The stuff hit the fan in August 1951. Football Coach Rube McCray and members of the coaching staff resigned after disclosure of corruption in the intercollegiate athletics program. Newspapers shredded W&M's reputation with stories — unfortunately quite true — of the way in which coaches, particularly in football, had broken academic rules and violated the honor code in order to enroll scholastically unqualified athletes and maintain their academic eligibility. Although not involved in the cheating — and had been prevented from learning about it — President Pomfret resigned because, as he told me, he should have made it his business to know what was going on.

The only positive outcome of the scandal was the determination of William and Mary people — alumni, staff and faculty — never to allow such a situation to occur again. As a result, the college's athletic programs today are among the best in the nation at every qualitative level. Its athletes in every sport are truly student-athletes. As of this writing, W&M graduated an impeccable 100% of its football players who entered the program in recent years. According to the NCAA, W&M's lofty academic standards are the best among all the nation's public universities.

Aggressive Admiral vs. Fractious Faculty

A not-so-positive outcome of the scandal was the development of a schism between the college faculty and its board of visitors, especially over its appointment of Rear Admiral Alvin D. Chandler to the W&M presidency in the fall of 1951, just a few months after Pomfret's departure. Members of the faculty were infuriated because they had not been consulted in his choice.

The board of visitors' action — as I found out later — was deliberate. If, as they discovered, there had been rumors on campus of dubious activities in the athletic department, they were sure members of the faculty must have suspected something. Why hadn't any of them spoken up?

Chandler, whose father, J.A.C. Chandler, was W&M president from 1919 to 1934, was a much-decorated Navy veteran who graduated from the Naval Academy after attending William and Mary. As the official history of the college put it, the board felt that Chandler's family ties to the college "and his demonstrated administrative and command abilities appeared to be an ideal combination to correct the problems caused by the athletic scandal and to control a fractious faculty."

The admiral arrived on campus with at least two strikes against him. First of all, Chandler entered enemy territory when he came to Williamsburg. W&M faculty members were local residents, our friends and neighbors. Their resentment of the board of visitors and its choice of president rubbed off on everyone, townspeople and students alike. Second, Chandler was an aggressive, no-nonsense man who had not the foggiest idea of how to deal with faculty members.

Since the campus seethed in almost constant bickering and controversy, President Chandler was often in the news. As a reporter, I called upon him often for information, statements and quotes — and I admit that in the beginning of our long relationship I was not prepared to like him. A couple of times we wound up shouting at one another. At the same time, faculty members continually fed me stories about his alleged mishandling of personnel, administrative or educational affairs.

These whistle-blowing faculty members gave me their information surreptitiously — mostly by phone, but sometimes during a meeting at night in the parking lot behind my office. When I asked if I could quote them, their invariable reply was a fervent "No!" All they'd allow was for me to use the information to get the story from another source.

It came to me gradually that the W&M president, as I put it to my managing editor, "couldn't go down the hall to the john without someone calling up to tell me about it."

The admiral never ducked a tough question. He gave me answers. They weren't always good answers — sometimes I went so far as to tell him so — but I could always use them in my stories. A day later, he might realize his mistake and issue a denial or a different statement to my competition. In such cases, the admiral and I might have a yelling match across his desk.

In the lulls between campus outbursts, I'd encounter him around town or on campus. One time he took me up into the attic of Rogers Hall and showed me a plaster model of the campus envisioned by his father. He said the main reason he had agreed to take on the job of W&M president was to try to fulfill his father's dream. It was a poignant moment, because I had been told that when his father, J.A.C. Chandler, was replaced as president in 1934 because of failing health, it was discovered that he had used some creative juggling of funds to finance his building program — not that he ever embezzled a penny. Apparently, he was just eager to get on with expanding the campus. The classic example of his inspired manipulation is the William and Mary football stadium, which was built with Federal funds as a cattle arena — hence the large opening and lack of seating at the fifty-yard line.

I came to respect Admiral Chandler. I'm glad I did, because I didn't learn until long after he was kicked upstairs to the job of chancellor that he had nominated me for the Young Man of the Year award I won. He wrote the nomination letter just a few days after one of our worst shouting matches.

The Fourth Estate

"I'm not sure who they hate more, me or the *Richmond Times-Dispatch*," I complained to State Editor Dick Carter, my boss.

When I began covering courthouses, attending supervisors' meetings and generally making myself known in the counties around Williamsburg, I was not welcomed with enthusiasm. In fact, my presence seemed to generate an undercurrent of hostility. Many county officials were reluctant to answer my questions. This was frustrating and made it difficult for me to get information I needed to write accurate stories.

Carter, with years of experience, grinned. "It's because before now they've never seen a reporter except when something bad happened. Then city reporters showed up, spent a couple hours skimming off the sensational stuff, then went back to their cities. Next day there'd be headlines and stories that usually made them or their county look bad."

"So I'm going to bat with two strikes," I said. "That makes it tough to get on base. What can I do?"

"Keep on attending their meetings, keep in touch with the courthouse folks, show them we're interested in them every day, not just when they have problems. They'll come around."

My boss was right, of course. I made it my business to build friendships with supervisors and officials in the counties assigned to me. In this process of gaining the trust and confidence of those folks, however, I may have violated a tenet of journalism.

I found out that those who held elective offices were mostly honest, conscientious older men — I rarely encountered a woman — who lived their entire lives in the districts they represented. Typically, they were farmers, watermen or merchants whose education rarely went beyond grammar school. This is not to say they were ignorant, for when it came to common sense, they sometimes put Williamsburg's well-educated councilmen to shame.

Unfortunately, they tended to be less articulate than people with more education and wider experience. When they spoke up in discussions or arguments, their language was so country and colloquial that I realized if I quoted them exactly they'd seem ignorant — and I knew they weren't.

So if I quoted them, I cleaned up their language.

A supervisor in New Kent, angry at the state highway department, might say, "Daggone road past Possum Creek got 'nuff potholes a jackass couldn't get by it." I'd rewrite it, "The Possum Creek road is in serious need of repair." Then I'd show it to the supervisor after the meeting. "Is this what you meant?" All he had to do was nod and that's what I'd print.

Or a supervisor in Mathews County might take issue with a reassessment: "Man don't know nothin' 'bout land here, dumb ass counts ol' Henry Hudgins' backyard like its pasture. Ain't got sense 'nuff to see it when it rains, then he'd hafta swim to cross it. And Ah hope he drowns." After my editing, it read, "I believe the assessor made a mistake on Mr. Henry Hudgins' farm. I think he had better take another look at it."

In every county there was continued skirmishing between the conservative supervisors and the school board. This produced complaints like the following from a supervisor in Charles City County: "Why we payin' fo' gas 'n' drivers an' usin' our buses to take kids sightseein' in Williamsburg? Seems to me we ain't teachin' them nothin' by givin' them days off like that." I changed it, with his approval, to, "With our limited budget, I believe we should concentrate on teaching our children in regular school classes."

Some years later, while having lunch at the National Press Club in Washington with some other former reporters, I talked about some of my experiences covering rural counties, including that I frequently rewrote direct quotations. One of the others, a former reporter for a Philadelphia newspaper, castigated me for 'doctoring' the quotes.

"You were acting as their press agent!" he accused me. "You wrote their statements."

Strictly speaking, he was right, but I'd do it again if necessary. The men I quoted were good men; I didn't have the heart to make them seem like morons.

James E. Mays

Times-Dispatch *reporter hard at work. Photo taken by competitor.*

Besides, within a few months, nothing important ever happened in those counties that I didn't immediately learn about from one or more of their officials. But the best part was to be greeted as a friend wherever I went.

My competition for news in the Williamsburg area was the *Newport News Daily Press*, which had a news bureau in Williamsburg staffed by long time reporter Lloyd Williams. I'll admit that I was never a great admirer of Williams, for he seemed always to represent and support positions exactly the opposite of mine. To make matters more difficult, he was a member of city council. When the council went into executive session, I was excluded but Williams wasn't.

After a couple of months of this, I told him I thought it was entirely unfair for him to be present for discussions of public business to which I was excluded. To my surprise, he agreed. After insisting that he never used any of the information he obtained in the executive sessions in his news stories, he said if I'd promise to do likewise, he would call me after every executive session and tell me exactly what transpired. I agreed. Until he lost his council seat he kept me informed.

Williams and I cooperated in another way, the gathering of election results. Although all of Williamsburg's voting took place in the South England Street Courthouse, James City residents voted in several precincts, a couple of which had no telephones. Lloyd Williams drove to one of them, I motored to the other. When we had all the numbers, we'd put them together so we'd both show the same tallies. It worked very nicely.

My election run was to Black Stump Precinct in the wilds of Powhatan District near the Chickahominy River. Seventeen men and women voted there on the porch of a farmhouse and usually all of them did so long before the polls closed, which permitted me to return to town early. I enjoyed the trip.

Black Stump is no longer a voting precinct, but the old farmhouse is still there on Jolly Pond Road. The former voting place, a small building, is beyond Jolly's Pond, on the left at the top of a twisting uphill drive.

Honest to a Fault

Like most young men and women who earned a college degree, I entered the postgraduate world like a shiny new nail, smugly secure in my great knowledge of the world in which I would live. It only took a couple of hammer blows to put me in my place. If I hadn't been lucky, I would have bent, become useless and been tossed out. I got the message early on: there's no substitute for experience.

Caroline had an aunt, Martha Lane, who married Ashton Dovell. They had a magnificent home on Scotland Street in Williamsburg. For many years a member of Virginia's General Assembly, Dovell became Speaker of the House of Delegates and in the years just before the outbreak of World War II was on track to be nominated for governor. But, as the story goes, he had the bad luck to disagree on an important issue with Virginia Senator Harry Flood Byrd. The result was political disaster for Dovell. He lost not only his opportunity to run for governor with the backing of the Byrd organization, but his seat in the General Assembly as well.

Thus, when given the opportunity in the 1950s to represent the *Richmond Times-Dispatch* in a relatively large area of Tidewater Virginia, I saw it as a way to explore the workings of Senator Byrd's organization and, if possible, shed journalistic light on its machinations. As I soon discovered, however, there was not a whole lot to discover about the Byrd organization — but a whole lot to learn about Virginia politics and government.

For many years, from the 1920s to 1950s, Senator Byrd and his network of allies were the political masters of Virginia. It was a given that any man with ambitions of becoming an elected officer in the Old Dominion had to have the blessing — and support — of what people called the Byrd Organization. (Some folks referred to it as the Byrd Machine.)

With a heritage of the Reconstruction years of the late 1800s still lingering in Virginia, it was the kiss of political death to be a Republican. Like Byrd himself, the candidates he endorsed were conservative Democrats.

I never stopped seeking the elusive secret of Byrd's political power and finally concluded that it was a product of the times. Virginia's election laws and customs of the era meant that only a small percentage of the population voted, and since the Republican vote was insignificant, nomination in the Democratic primary was tantamount to election.

County courthouses were the keystones of Byrd's power, but not for graft or underhanded deals. As far as I could determine, it was a case of like-thinking men in the courthouse crowd agreeing who was best suited for a specific elective office and uniting in his support. Byrd wanted conservative, loyal men in political offices. Above all else, they had to be honest. This was to the good, but some of the most honest and trustworthy officeholders I dealt with were not rocket scientists. I think it's safe to say that the Byrd organization tolerated some slow thinkers.

Chapter Six

Public Safety

During the postwar years in Williamsburg we seldom had to look very far for a policeman. The town's only police vehicle was almost always parked on Duke of Gloucester Street in front of Steve Sacalis' Williamsburg Restaurant, with officers Ham Smith or his brother Llew leaning against it. (Incidentally, Ham was an abbreviation for Hamlet, Llew for Llewellyn.)

Folks who didn't know any better were inclined to criticize our policemen for spending so much of their time hanging out near College Corner, but there was a valid reason. For many years, the police didn't have a radio. If someone wanted the police, the call went to the telephone company switchboard located on the second floor above Peninsula Hardware, the building next door to the restaurant. To get word to the police, the operator simply opened a window and yelled down to whomever was on duty.

If by some chance the police vehicle was not in its usual spot, the telephone operator had means of turning on a light located on the city water tower near the railroad station. When away from College Corner, the officers were supposed to keep an eye on the tower. If the light came on, they'd go to a phone to find out what was needed.

When the city equipped its fire and police vehicles with radios, a man was always on duty at the old South Henry Street firehouse to take emergency calls. That made it unnecessary for the police to continue to park at College Corner, but the habit was so thoroughly ingrained that their spot in front of the Corner Greek's remained the unofficial police station until that part of Duke of Gloucester Street was closed to traffic.

Through a freak of atmospheric 'bounce' the early long-wave radios we used in Williamsburg often provided better communication

Newport News Daily Press

College Corner in the 1950s. Police cruiser and Officer Ham Smith visible at far left in usual location in front of what was known as the 'Corner Greek's,' officially the Williamsburg Restaurant owned and operated by Steve Sacalis.

with Baton Rouge, Louisiana, than with local units. It was eerie to call headquarters from our ambulance and get a reply from a guy with a Deep South drawl — and at least once, while local volunteers were fighting a fire, the Baton Rouge dispatcher heard the talk between our units and kept up with our progress with frequent questions.

Crime in our area was virtually non-existent during those post-war years, which was fortunate, for police protection was minimal. In Williamsburg, the Smith brothers and three or four other men constituted Chief W.H. Kelly's entire force. York County's Sheriff White and his deputies were generally too busy at the lower end of their county to pay much attention to Bruton District, the area around Williamsburg.

James City had only Sheriff Wayne Lovelace and a single deputy to protect the entire county — and Lovelace was primarily an officer of the court, not a law enforcer. County sheriffs were elected. Thus Lovelace, who loved publicity, put a lot of effort into maintaining a high public profile. As a reporter, I received his special attention. For example, when he discovered I didn't have a pistol to protect my home and family, he gave me one. When I protested that I'd never used a pistol, he took me to a ravine near Chickahominy Church, produced a box of ammunition, and taught me how to shoot.

One winter Lovelace arranged for the loan of a helicopter from the Army Transportation Corps at Fort Eustis. His purpose, he explained, was to fly over the woods and swamps bordering the Chickahominy River seeking stills, because moonshining was a cottage industry in the upper county. He invited me to go along so I could write a story about it for the *Times-Dispatch.*

The helicopter was a piston-engined H-19, which seated three — warrant officer pilot in the middle, Lovelace on the right and me on the left. I met them on a cold, crisp January day at the old College Airport at Ewell and off we went. We reached the search area within a few minutes at an altitude of little more than a thousand feet, but we didn't do much looking before the motor quit. (Later we discovered that the carburetor had iced up.)

Fortunately, the helicopter blades continued to spin and provide some lift as we descended rapidly toward the unbroken forest. There was no question that we'd be in deep trouble when the blades splintered against the tops of the trees. With only moments to spare, I caught sight of a tiny clearing on my side of the 'copter and pointed it out to the pilot. He must have been very good at his job, for he managed to put us down — very heavily — in a bush-laden field not much larger than a tennis court. So we survived, but I've never been comfortable in a helicopter since then.

That's one of the few times I neglected to report a legitimate story — because I didn't want Caroline to know I'd done anything dangerous — so Sheriff Lovelace didn't get the publicity he sought in the *Times-Dispatch.*

Fortunately for rural areas, the Virginia State Police maintained an area office in Williamsburg. The handful of troopers assigned here took on much of the police work in the counties — and of course were always on the scene at automobile accidents. Over the years, our rescue squad responded to hundreds of accidents in Williamsburg, James City or upper York County where people were injured or killed, so we worked closely with the troopers.

One of hundreds of rescues.
(From left) *late at night on a typical run, volunteers Gene Mason and Selby Jacobs, and Chief Elliott Jayne carry an accident victim to our ambulance.*

I'm sure that when we decided to fill the need for a rescue squad, many of our volunteer firemen, though basically conscientious and happy to be of service to the community, were intrigued by the prospect of the excitement and adventure it offered. It did not take long for some of the eager volunteers to realize that dealing with dead and/or mangled human beings was not something they could cope with.

Many of us, however, learned to deal with death, trauma and horror, to do our best to patch up and splint lacerated, bloody bodies. When we began there were no instruction manuals beyond the Red Cross advanced first aid handbook. We learned from experience and from advice provided by emergency room doctors. I know that in our early days we probably lost victims we might have saved if we'd known more, but in later years we actually saved lives — and nothing is more satisfying.

Many of us found we were able to face the horrors of human wreckage and deaths we encountered, particularly in responding to highway accidents. But we didn't realize that those of us who could handle that blood, gore and filth operated on a thin layer of tolerance. I was one of those who believed we could handle any kind of trauma and misery — but I was wrong. There was a limit.

Trooper Lonnie Craft wasn't even on duty when he showed us that limit. One evening our rescue squad responded to a single-vehicle accident on old Route 168 (now Rochambeau Road). The car had run into a large tree. The two volunteers who were dispatched in the ambulance radioed for backup help, so several of us rode to the scene, just beyond the Camp Peary entrance, with Trooper Craft, who happened to be at the fire station.

We patched up the driver and his wife as best we could and got them into the ambulance quickly, for the woman had lost most of one leg and a lot of blood. To save her life, our ambulance had to get her to Newport News' Riverside Hospital as fast as possible.

After the ambulance left, Val Pitts arrived with his wrecker to remove the battered automobile. First thing he did was lift its mangled front end from the tree. To our horror, as the car rose we saw the woman's severed leg dangling from the transmission. Pitts, standing beside his controls, yelled, "Somebody get that thing off so I can move the damn car."

There must have been four or five volunteer firemen there, but nobody moved. We just looked at one another. Although all had dealt with trauma and corpses, none wanted to touch that leg. I went so far as to pick up my Speed Graphic to provide an excuse for not doing so.

Then Trooper Craft asked, "Anybody got a bag?"

Pitts had one and gave it to him. Craft put on a pair of gloves and quickly removed the leg. I was able to take a photograph as he did so. That's as close as I wanted to get to the thing — then or ever. Like the other volunteers there that night, I'd reached the limit of my tolerance of horror.

Our tolerance of horror had a limit. State Trooper Lonnie Craft, off duty, prepares to remove woman's severed leg from wrecked automobile when rescue squad volunteers declined the opportunity.

A few years later, when the state police established a plain-clothes investigation branch, Trooper Craft applied for a transfer and was accepted. So was Trooper Dave Jones, another of the men who spent several years in the Williamsburg area office. Dave had a rosy, cherubic face that made him look as if he were an innocent teen playing at being a state trooper. Although he was an effective law enforcement officer, I discovered one summer Saturday afternoon that he really did have a streak of innocence.

Caroline and our first-born were at the beach with her mother. I planned to join her as soon as I finished teletyping a story to the *Times-Dispatch* about results of an important statewide gathering being held at the Williamsburg Lodge. To kill time until the meeting ended, I hung out with some friends at the fire station.

Trooper Jones pulled into our ramp, got a nickel bottle of Coca-Cola and told us he was out "showing the flag" in weekend traffic. He invited me to ride with him (I don't think this was strictly legal, but in those days troopers occasionally carried reporters and other VIPs as passengers). I hopped into his cruiser and he drove up Route 60 all the way to Diascund Bridge, turned around and headed back toward Williamsburg.

As we approached Anderson's Corner, a car came speeding up Route 60 from Toano and, without slowing down, flew across the highway and up Route 30 toward West Point. There were no traffic lights at the intersection in those days, but there was a large stop sign. Dave sighed, turned on his red lights and pursued the errant car. He caught up to it within a quarter mile and sounded his siren. The driver pulled off the road and stopped. Dave parked right behind it. As he got out of his cruiser, he told me, "I've got to write a summons."

From my seat, I heard Dave tell the driver he wanted to see the operator's license and car registration. As he leaned toward the driver's open window, his face turned a deep shade of red. He mumbled, "Yes, ma'am." Then he took a step back, adjusted his Stetson and threw me a look of distress.

The driver — a young woman — left the vehicle, went to its trunk (right in front of where I sat in the cruiser), fished around in some bags and found what she sought — her operator's license. She handed it to Dave. I think he looked at it, but I'll never know for sure. He hurriedly returned it to her and told her, "Next time you do something like that, I'll have to issue a summons."

"Thank you, sir! I'll be good." The woman returned to her car, started up and drove off. Dave remained rooted to the spot, face still flushed. The woman hadn't been naked, but she might as well have been, for her only attire was a see-through nightgown or some similar invisible fabric. Her figure, totally visible, was magnificent. Dave was still talking about it many years later.

Tom Fisher was the state trooper who served in the Williamsburg area the longest. A former professional baseball player, he was immensely strong. Some of the feats of strength he displayed in helping us deal with accident victims were almost unbelievable, like the time he single-handedly peeled back the roof of a pickup truck so I could get into the cab and remove a pregnant woman. But that's not what I remember best about him, for Tom figured in a rescue squad odyssey I experienced with Skip Smith.

In the days before Busch Gardens, Route 60 between Williamsburg and Grove was a simple two-lane highway which crossed the James City–York County boundary three or four times. Opposite what's now a huge Busch parking lot, beside the C&O tracks, was a logging operation. One night, two of the men who worked and lived there went down to Grove to relax. Walking back up the highway too drunk to be careful, they were hit by a couple of vehicles.

About midnight, Skip Smith and I responded to the scene. Two bloody bodies lay in the middle of Route 60. Trooper Fisher was already on the scene and there was a growing crowd of spectators. We parked the ambulance close to the victims and checked the first one. He was obviously dead.

The second man was alive but unconscious. We bandaged him as best we could and splinted broken limbs. Fisher helped us lift him from the road and place him on a stretcher. As we slid it into the ambulance, he asked us, "Aren't you going to pick up the other one?"

We told Tom the guy was dead, that we couldn't move him without an okay from the medical examiner.

"I've got to get traffic moving again and I can't do it with that body right in the middle of the road. Besides, the natives are getting restless. They can't understand why y'all haven't done anythin' for that man," he said. "Do me a favor and pick him up. Anyway, you can't be all that sure he's dead, can you?"

Skip and I exchanged shrugs. We liked Tom too much to turn him down, so we grabbed one of our lightweight stretchers. We made a tactical error, however. The dead man was on his back on the highway. We simply rolled him onto the stretcher, so he was lying face down. When we hung the stretcher from roof hooks inside the ambulance, the toes of his shoes hung down in the rear window. Then we took off, headed for Riverside Hospital in downtown Newport News.

When we backed down the ramp leading to the emergency room, hospital staff members helped us get the living patient inside. When we began to unhook the hanging stretcher, the night nursing supervisor stopped us.

She knew we weren't supposed to load patients face down. She reached into the ambulance and felt the man's leg, which, of course, was icy. She shook her head at us. "Uh-uh. You don't unload this one."

I shrugged. "Okay, we'll take him back to Williamsburg."

She shook her head again. "No, you won't. You won't move him from here without an okay from the medical examiner."

"Who's the medical examiner for Newport News?" Skip asked. "We'll call him."

"That won't work, either." The nurse closed the ambulance door. "I have to have an okay from the medical examiner of the county he died in. Otherwise, I'll call the police to keep y'all here."

Trooper Fisher's told us what happened next. A phone call from the Norfolk divisional office of the state police awoke him. He was told to determine the county in which our victim had died, contact the medical examiner of that county, and have him call Riverside Hospital so the Williamsburg Fire Department Rescue Squad could return its ambulance to the station. Tom told us there was no way he could have determined whether the man died in James City or York Counties. "But I did know the medical examiners. I knew from experience the one for James City wouldn't even answer his phone at that time of night, but that the younger guy in York County would be cooperative."

So Riverside Hospital was advised by the York County examiner to release the accident victim. Accordingly, at about two in the morning,

Skip and I were able to start back toward Williamsburg with the corpse still hanging face down in the back of the ambulance.

By this time, we were both sleepy and hungry, so we decided to stop at an all-night doughnut shop at the intersection leading to the James River Bridge. To be safe, we parked in front of a plate glass window where we could keep an eye on the ambulance. The little restaurant was crowded with young couples in formal wear. They'd obviously come from a high school dance. Skip and I drank some strong coffee and ate a couple of doughnuts, then headed toward the ambulance.

A group of boys and girls, grouped around its rear window, were arguing: "It's a dead man!" "No, it couldn't be!" "It is so!"

When we approached, one girl, holding her long formal gown so that it wouldn't drag in the dirt, asked Skip, "Is that really a dead body?"

Skip nodded. "Yep, sure is."

"I don't believe it!" she replied.

My buddy glanced at me, shrugged, then opened the rear door wide enough to see our passenger. The girl took a quick look and threw up, messing up her pretty ball gown.

A bit after three-thirty in the morning we turned into the driveway of the Whiting and Tabb Funeral Home, which used to be on York Street where CW now pastures some horses. Old Mr. Whiting, in pajamas and bathrobe, came out of the house and opened the door of the outbuilding where he embalmed his customers.

Skip and I carried the stretcher inside. Whiting reached across his treatment table and flopped the corpse upon it.

I frowned. "Mr. Whiting, you treated that man kind of rough."

With great dignity, he straightened up, looked me in the eye and said, "Son, the man is gone."

Yankee Fireball

In March 1950, one visitor died and another was badly burned in a fire at Brick House Tavern on Duke of Gloucester Street, a subsidiary of the Williamsburg Lodge. The city's volunteer firemen of that date exhibited a number of shortcomings in their attempts to fight the blaze. Many of their faults were attributed to lack of training and leadership.

The need to provide better fire protection for both residents and visitors brought prompt and gratifying cooperation between city council and Colonial Williamsburg. Together they took immediate action. Although the city was too small to afford a fully professional department, they agreed to share the expense of employing a professional training officer to take charge of the fire department with emphasis upon upgrading the quality and training of its volunteer firefighters.

City and CW worked through the New York office of Mr. Rockefeller and found a young fire training officer from New York. On July 1, 1950, Elliott W. Jayne went to work in the old fire station on Henry Street. His title was 'Marshal', although he functioned as chief. He had two paid employees, men who worked alternating 24-hour shifts handling both fire and police phone calls.

He inherited three pieces of equipment. The city's pride was a recently acquired 1948 Mack 750 gallon-per-minute pumper. Unfortunately, when the city prepared invitations for bidding on the engine, the former volunteer officers were unable to provide any specifications except "get one like they have in Richmond". This meant that the shiny new vehicle — designated Engine One — was perfectly equipped for fighting big city fires but not particularly suited for Williamsburg. Engine Two was an underpowered 1941 Ford Oren 500 gallon-per-minute pumper. The third unit was a 1936 LaSalle ambulance acquired from Navy surplus. When we tried to operate it, we discovered why it was declared surplus.

Undeterred by shortcomings in equipment, Jayne began by cleaning house. Only a few pre-1950 volunteers survived his screening. It wasn't merely because he insisted on high standards of character and intelligence. He not only told the volunteers he expected them to respond to all fire calls but to report every Monday night for training. "On Monday nights, your ass belongs to me!"

Jayne spent the summer of 1950 actively recruiting his kind of volunteer — men who weren't afraid of the challenge he posed. He received significant help not only from the city and CW but from the power and phone companies and local merchants. He wanted and obtained the services of about forty volunteers, a number he maintained throughout his twelve years as chief, adding new men as needed to

Chief Elliott Jayne's Original Volunteers and Invited Guests
First Annual Banquet, May 1951

1) Harry Moss, 2) Floyd Martin, 3) Jack Bailey, 4) Billy Morecock, 5) Dusty Rhodes, 6) unidentified, 7) Kenneth Briggs, 8) Hugh Hitchens, 9) Joe Fish, 10) Willis Burton, 11) author, 12) Skip Smith, 13) Bill Hodge, 14) Bill Landon, 15) Charles Hackett, 16) Bill Schreiber, 17) Fletcher Cox, 18) Pop Summers, 19) Carl Madison, 20) Kemper Taylor,

21) Chief W.H. Kelly, 22) Rev. Archie Ward, 23) John Norwood, 24) Frank Edwards, 25) Fred Mayfield, 26) Paul Angel, 27) Dan Bradley, 28) Hank Ertl, 29) Elliott Jayne, 30) Peanut Haynes, 31) John Epperson, 32) Monier Williams, 33) Alvin Robertson, 34) Dean Nelson Marshall, 35) Bela Norton, 36) Dr. Granville Jones, 37) Judge Frank Armistead, 38) Winston Butts, 39) Mayor Polly Stryker, 40) Bob Holmes, 41) Dick Lawson, 42) Lloyd Williams, 43) Hugh Rice, 44) Charles F. Marsh, 45) Vincent McManus, 46) John Hedgebeth, 47) Al Liptow, 48) Teeny Hodge, 49) Elmer Farthing, 50) John Flanagan, 51) Herb Gordon, 52) Frank Epperson. The City of Williamsburg was represented by Mayor Stryker; Vice Mayor Williams; councilmen Butts, Marsh and MacManus; City Manager Rice; and Police Chief Kelly. Others in attendance were CW Vice President Norton, Eastern State Hospital Superintendent Dr. Jones, William and Mary Dean Marshall and Circuit Court Judge Armistead; James City's Volunteer Fire Department's Taylor (Toano), Madison (Lightfoot) and Summers (Ewell). Holmes was retired chief of the Williamsburg Department and Fletcher Cox represented The Virginia Gazette. *The Reverend Archie Ward offered the invocation.*

fill vacancies. His volunteers ranged from an illiterate to a Ph.D., and included everything from laborers to a CW vice president.

Under Jayne's progressive, aggressive teaching, the volunteers learned and used cutting-edge firefighting techniques and were among the first volunteer firemen in America to employ home radio sets for night alarms. Instead of waking the whole town with sirens atop the city water tower and fire station, between 7 p.m. and 7 a.m. the volunteers were summoned by radio. The wail of sirens continued to be used during the day when most volunteers were at work.

In the fall of 1950, the new volunteers painted their old LaSalle ambulance a bright red and began responding to emergencies. It was the beginning of the city's Rescue Squad, now Emergency Medical Service. When the old ambulance shorted out and died on Route 60 in front of the Pottery, they enlisted local help — including the United Fund — to finance a new ambulance. To increase its visibility, they had it painted white. All equipment acquired since then has been basically white. (The old 1948 Mack pumper, kept in operating condition as a reserve pumper by today's firemen, retains its original red color.)

The Bucks Stopped There

Just about the last thing I ever contemplated was becoming a volunteer fireman. But that was before I met Elliott Jayne.

In the spring of 1950, Horace "Hunky" Henderson, president of the local Jaycee organization — and later its national president — persuaded me to join the club. I'd been putting him off as long as I was employed at the Inn and Lodge because of the irregularity of my work hours, but I had just gone to work at the W&M alumni office, so I agreed on one condition. I had learned that every Jaycee had to become chairman of some committee, so I told Hunky I'd join up if he gave me an easy one. He did. He made me chairman of October's Fire Prevention Week.

"There's a new fire chief coming in July," Hunky told me. "Go see him around the first of August. I betcha he'll take most of the responsibility."

So one afternoon shortly after the first of August, I visited the Henry Street fire station and met Marshal Jayne. He invited me upstairs into his

Neighbor's home destroyed. When Chief Jayne arrived in town, the city of Williamsburg did not have the responsibility for fires in neighboring James City and York Counties or the necessary equipment, but Williamsburg volunteers used their own funds to purchase a small truck with limited firefighting capability for use outside the city. Thus the best that volunteers Dickie Gilliam (left) *and Norwood Singleton could do with this conflagration on Penniman Road was prevent its spreading to neighboring homes.*

office. I'm not sure exactly what happened after that, but when I went back downstairs about thirty minutes later, I was a volunteer in the Williamsburg Fire Department. Caroline didn't believe me at first. Neither did Hunky Henderson when I resigned from the Jaycees. After listening to Jayne, I knew I'd have no time for anything but the fire department.

We actually were paid by the city. A hangover from older times, when money was more valuable and volunteers harder to come by, the city paid each man one dollar for every fire to which he responded. For some reason, the old rule was never rescinded. Jayne kept a record of who responded to fire calls and every three months, the city conveyed a check to be distributed to individual volunteers according to the number of fire calls we answered.

None of us ever accepted a penny of those city payments. Every time a check arrived, we voted unanimously to use all of it for the purchase of equipment. That, in addition to the marvelous fellowship we enjoyed and the service we performed, built the immense pride we all feel today for our years as volunteers.

From mid-August 1950 until the spring of 1958, it was a rare Monday night that I missed a training session. Jayne started us at ground zero with lectures on the chemistry of fire. Our classroom was a large room on the second floor of the fire station on South Henry Street, where the Seasons Arcade is now located. When not used for lectures, it was our recreation room, complete with pool table and a brass pole down which we slid if there was a fire call.

Most Monday nights, Jayne had us outdoors in turnout clothing, drilling us in all kinds of firefighting functions because, as he told us, when reporting to a fire, we had to recognize what needed to be done and then be able to do it. We not only learned how to use nozzles and hoses, we had to learn to operate the pumpers, use breathing apparatus and work in smoke-filled buildings. (We were also schooled in the use of ladders, but I managed to avoid that part of our training.)

Although he insisted on our working as safely as possible, he made it clear that there would be times when we'd have to take risks. He built a pit, then collected old crankcase oil from filling stations to provide fires

---

(Right): *Phi Beta Kappa Memorial Hall, 8:15 p.m., December 29, 1953. As I triggered the camera, the auditorium roof fell in. A huge ball of fire erupted.*

for us to drill on. As we acquired some skills, he had us practice on real buildings such as college dormitories, Eastern State Hospital buildings, the Governor's Palace and, most importantly, Phi Beta Kappa Memorial Hall, a college structure Jayne described as a building designed to burn.

Graduation Night at Phi Beta Kappa Hall

The William and Mary campus is deserted between Christmas and New Year's. Students are away on holiday break, and because the heat is turned off in its buildings, faculty members are not apt to use their offices. The national headquarters of the Phi Beta Kappa Society,

Not state-of-the-art technique.
In fighting the Phi Beta Kappa Hall fire Billy Morecock throws a brick in an effort to break a window on the balcony staircase which was interfering with hose streams. Identifiable at left are Booby Gore, who didn't take time to don turnout gear, and George Merriam.

occupying the second floor of the wing of Phi Beta Kappa Memorial Hall nearest the Sunken Gardens, was deserted. There was no one to watch over its irreplaceable records.

About eight o'clock on the evening of December 27, 1953, a young man driving into town on Jamestown Road noticed an orange glow inside the Phi Beta Kappa Hall auditorium. He hastened to the fire station to report it.

I was attending a meeting at the Williamsburg Inn when the town fire siren began wailing. I ran to my car and sped up Francis Street to the firehouse. Engine One, our big Mack pumper was gone, but the station doors were open and the duty fireman had scrawled 'Phi Beta Kappa Hall' on the blackboard that provided the volunteers with a fire's location.

Engine Two, our Ford pumper, was in its place. No one else was around, so I threw my camera into the front seat and drove up Jamestown road to Phi Bete as fast as it would move. Engine One was positioned close to the building adjacent to the stage. Smoke jetted from the auditorium eaves as if under great pressure.

As we'd practiced several times, I placed Engine Two beside a hydrant next to the Sunken Garden in front of Phi Bete. As fast as I could, I connected to the hydrant, paused for a moment to don some turnout clothes, then grabbed my Speed Graphic, ran to the small parking area near Jamestown Road and focused on the building. As I triggered the camera, the auditorium roof fell in. A huge ball of fire erupted. (Friends in West Point, twenty miles away, told me later that they saw it.)

By the time I ran back to Engine Two the auditorium had became a huge, roaring bonfire. The old aerial ladder, which we'd bought from New Haven for seventy-five dollars, rumbled past me, en route to a location on the Washington Hall side of Phi Bete. I scrambled to lay out hose to supply its ladder pipe. Other volunteers arrived. Several pitched in to help.

Elliott Jayne appeared.

"Are we gonna save Washington Hall?" I asked him, figuring the Phi Beta Kappa building was doomed.

He gave me a disgusted look. "We're gonna do better than that!"

Before I could react, he continued, "We've put a ladder up to the front windows of the Phi Beta Kappa offices. Get three guys from your company and take a line up there. Go to the balcony entrance and keep the fire from getting into the offices!"

There was absolutely no way I would ever have done it on my own. The conflagration was scary. Huge leaping flames from the auditorium were illuminating the whole campus. Secondly, I suffer from acrophobia. In all my career as a volunteer fireman I always managed to avoid ladder work. Climbing more than a foot or two above the ground turned me into Jello.

Then I saw Chief Jayne's expression. Facing the fear of fire and perils of climbing a ladder suddenly became preferable to experiencing his wrath.

The morning after: December 30, 1953.
Chief Elliott W. Jayne stands in what was a balcony exit from the Phi Beta Kappa Memorial Hall auditorium. It led to the area which housed the national headquarters of the Phi Beta Kappa Society. Williamsburg's volunteer firemen stopped the fire from spreading beyond this point.

I found three guys, got a hose and somehow managed to climb the ladder to the offices. Then we spent a couple of hair-raising hours preventing the flames from invading the headquarters of the Phi Beta Kappa Society. Its irreplaceable records suffered neither fire nor water damage.

We weren't the only Williamsburg volunteers fighting the conflagration, of course. Men with the aerial ladder kept the flames from the attic over our heads and others used their hoses both on the first floor below us — and the crawl space below that — to protect the unburned end of Phi Beta Kappa Hall. For a long time afterward I confess to having bragged about my experiences, describing how the whole building shook as we fought to keep the flames in check.

von Dubell Photo

After more than two years of Chief Jayne's training, the 1953 Williamsburg Fire Department Volunteers: (From left, standing) *Gene Mason, Norwood Singleton, Ed Hall, Selby Jacobs, John Hedgebeth, Joe Fish, Roy Tait, Tom Russell, unidentified, Frank Epperson, Paul Angel, Hank Ertl, John Epperson, Roy McConnell, Charlie Hackett.* (Kneeling) *George Merriam, John Flanagan, Dickie Gilliam, unidentified, Bob Stubblefield, Harry Moss, Elliott Jayne & our mascot 'Fog', Alvin Robertson, Bill Miller, Dick Lawson, Dave Orr, Booby Gore, Dusty Rhodes, author.*

A few years ago Gene Mason, one of the volunteers who was with me in the Phi Beta Kappa offices that night, heard me.

"Fred," he said, "the building wasn't shaking."

"It sure was," I insisted. "I can still feel it."

He shook his head. "Nope. It wasn't the building. It was you."

When Jayne left Williamsburg in 1962, the department had developed into a largely paid, professional organization. The exploits of his volunteers were featured in two national magazines. *Argosy* carried an article about their firefighting exploits and *True Adventure* featured their Rescue Squad experiences. *Fire Engineering,* the professional journal of firefighters, printed a flattering article about the excellent work of the Williamsburg volunteers in saving irreplaceable records of the Phi Beta Kappa Society during the fire which was our graduation into the ranks of honest-to-goodness firefighters.

Chapter Seven

Virginia's Not-So-Distant Past

I didn't recognize it for what it was at the time, but I encountered a living artifact from Virginia's past in July 1942, soon after arriving in Williamsburg. Together with a couple of hundred other young men who had enrolled in William and Mary's War Work Program, I was sent to work at Naval Mine Depot as a laborer. A superintendent split us into groups of fifteen or twenty and placed each group under the direction of an experienced leading laborer.

My bunch was put in the care of Willie Hogge, a large middle-aged man more than six feet tall. He wore bib overalls and a straw hat. At first he seemed tongue-tied, but after staring at us for a minute or two, he began to talk. He might as well have been speaking Chinese, for I couldn't understand a word he uttered. Neither, I quickly discovered, could boys who were native Virginians.

Mr. Bryant, the superintendent, hadn't left. A couple of us ran over to his pickup truck and explained that we couldn't understand Mr. Hogge.

Bryant broke up in laughter, then apologized. "I should have known better. Willie's a good worker, but he's from Guinea. They speak a language of their own. I'll get someone else."

I didn't have a chance to learn anything more about Guinea from Bryant, but over the years, especially while working as a reporter, I picked up stray bits of information. There's no secret about Guinea's location. It's across the York River in Gloucester County in a swampy, watery area at its southeastern tip, beyond a hamlet called Achilles. It was isolated until early in the 1900s, and strangers weren't welcome, so not much was known about it — except that its men supported their families by fishing, crabbing and tonging oysters. Over the years Guinea watermen established areas of Mobjack Bay as their fishing grounds and protected them fiercely from intrusion by outsiders (an old Mathews County waterman told me that men from Guinea didn't hesitate to shoot at interlopers, that he and his friends steered clear of Guinea waters).

But there doesn't seem any definitive answer to the mystery of where Guinea people came from or how they developed their puzzling language. Even men and women who are today's descendants of old Guinea can't enlighten us. There are, however, many explanations. The one I like best — and which seems to make sense — claims there were only six original family names in Guinea: Deal, Green, Hogge, Jenkins, Smith and West. A college professor told me many years ago that, as a hobby, he traced the six names back to a single regiment in Cornwallis' army at Yorktown. In those days English regiments were recruited in local areas and then, as now, there were as many different local dialects as there were regions of England. Thus the six soldiers must have all used the same kind of language, but a dialect different from soldiers in other regiments.

My professor said he had no idea whether the six soldiers deserted the British army or escaped capture by the French and Americans. In any case, they hid and made homes in the trackless swamps at the edge of Mobjack Bay. The real mystery, however, is where they found women to accompany them. Without them, Guinea would never have survived.

Their unique language probably developed unhindered during the nearly 150 years they were isolated. Men and women who are descendants of Guinea natives tell me the original Guinea tongue is rapidly disappearing, that only a few older folks still speak it. I sincerely hope someone has recorded it so future generations can hear it. In any case, I'm glad I heard Willie Hogge speak it, even if I couldn't understand what he said. His speech was a living artifact.

When told that my *Times-Dispatch* beat would include Charles City County, I confess that I was not enthused. What little I knew of that county, lying between James City and Richmond's outskirts, led me to believe it was little more than a blank spot in the map of Virginia — and I suspect there were many Williamsburg and Tidewater residents who agreed. Aside from a couple of famous plantation homes on the banks of the James River, there was little to suggest that it contained a treasure trove of Virginia history.

My education began almost immediately, and in explosive fashion.

I had a mandate to find stories which would increase the *T-D*'s readership in Charles City. Knowing that farming was one of its two big industries (the other was timbering), I visited the farm agent in Providence Forge and asked him to recommend the best farmer in Charles City. Without hesitation, he said, "Stanley Hula. He's at Sandy Point."

Subsequently I discovered that the Hulas were one of six Czechoslovak families who emigrated to this country around 1900. After a stab at farming in Kansas, they found better land in Henrico and Charles City counties. I don't know all the other family names, but in addition to the Hulas, I was told there were Kormans, Zuzmas and Ukrops, the latter the well-known name of a chain of supermarkets.

I looked up Stanley Hula and was able to write a feature story about him and his venture into crop irrigation — an innovation in those days — which was printed on the front page of the *T-D*'s Sunday Magazine. I liked Stanley. He wasn't a big man, but he was whip-leather tough and a workaholic. He had to be to deal with the demands of a couple of thousand acres.

He and his wife, Zora, had a small house on the shore of the James River. From time to time, I visited him. If I didn't find him out in the fields, I found him in his barn. We'd go down to the river to sit on his porch and drink ice water.

One day I notice a large cannon ball Stanley used as a doorstop. When I asked him about it, he told me he'd plowed it up some two or three years before and kept it as a souvenir. Having heard somewhere that old cannon balls might be dangerous, I suggested it might be smart if he had an expert check it. "If you don't mind, I'll ask the public information officer at Fort Eustis to send someone up here to make sure it won't blow up."

Stanley agreed and he met us a week or two later, when I led an Army six-by-six truck to his home. It contained a young soldier as driver and a master sergeant, the explosives expert.

I didn't see the cannon ball on the porch. "Where is it?" I asked.

"The weather turned cold," Stanley replied, "so I took it inside."

Sure enough, it was sitting on the floor beside a roaring fireplace.

The master sergeant turned pale. "My God! It's a Civil War mortar shell loaded with black powder. Everybody get out of the house!" He very gingerly picked up the cannon ball, rushed from the house and placed it on the beach.

Rejoining us, he shook his head. "I'll never understand why that thing didn't go off long ago. The powder they used is very unstable."

I asked how a mortar shell could end up on Hula's farm. The sergeant said that when the Union army retreated to Harrison's Landing on the James River after the Battle of Malvern Hill, it was supplied by ships sailing from Hampton Roads. Occasionally, the Confederates would tow a field gun to a riverside location and fire at the ships. The Yankee naval vessels fired back, often with mortars because the Rebels usually hid behind earthworks and mortars provided plunging fire. They had fuses like today's firecrackers. Gunners had to guess how long to make the fuse so the shell would explode at the right moment. A fuse cut too long and still burning when the shell hit the ground might be extinguished if the shell buried itself in the earth.

"What should I do with it?" Stanley asked.

"Nothing," the sergeant said. "I'm going to blow it up."

He dug a hole in the sand of the beach, attached a detonator and then shepherded us to what he figured was a safe place about a hundred feet away. I got my Speed Graphic camera and we all hunkered down behind a small sand dune. I aimed the camera. The sergeant triggered the detonator.

A huge explosion ensued. We should have been at least a hundred feet farther away, for we were showered with sand and debris. Worst of all, I was too close to get a meaningful photo. The explosion filled the frame. I might just as well have been shooting in a coal mine without light.

Dick Carter, the state editor, consoled me with, "Just think, you've had a contact with Virginia history!"

I soon had another such contact. It wasn't quite as violent as the mortar shell, but it shook me nonetheless.

Malcolm Jamieson, known as Mac, owned Berkeley, one of the James River plantations that attract tourists. Mac was an unashamed promoter and seeker of publicity — not for himself, but for his beautiful, historic home at Harrison's Landing, which dated to the years soon after Jamestown was settled. After the Battle of Malvern Hill, when the Union army barricaded itself at Harrison's Landing, Berkeley became a hospital and headquarters of General McClellan. It was at Berkeley that the bugle call "Taps" was composed and first sounded.

One day Mac saw me at the Charles City courthouse and urged me to take a ride out to his home to see something his son had unearthed. He wouldn't elaborate, so I made the trip to find out what it was. Mac took me down into the large cellar and indicated some strange objects lying on a table. They looked like gray wads of partly chewed bubble gum. I picked one up, surprised at its heavy weight.

"My boy was using a metal detector and found them outside the dining room window," Mac said. He paused for effect, then added, "They used the dining room as a surgery after Malvern Hill. When they sawed off a man's leg, they gave him a bullet to bite. Those are teeth marks you're looking at."

As I looked at those pieces of lead, I could only think that those poor soldiers must have hurt like hell — and had immensely strong teeth.

When I began covering Charles City, Lyon Tyler was its commonwealth's attorney. As such, he was present for meetings of the board of supervisors, which in those days were held in the office of the clerk of courts. Lyon was a classmate of mine at William and Mary. I had learned a little about the history of the college, including the fact that the president of the institution from 1888 to 1919 was Lyon G. Tyler. Not knowing any better, I asked Lyon if there was a connection. There was, of course. The man who served as W&M president for thirty-one years was his father. And there was more. I also learned that Lyon's grandfather had also been a president — of the United States — John Tyler.

Lyon had a younger brother, Harrison. They grew up just a few miles from Williamsburg at Sherwood Forest, the family home. Harrison had several claims to fame other than being grandson of a U.S. president. One was the fact that he was the last man to date my wife, Caroline, before I became her steady beau. But his eye for beauty never weakened. He married a lovely Southern belle named Payne (pronounced Paynee).

But as much as I liked and admired the Tylers, their connection with U.S. President Tyler did not bring Virginia history as close to me as did an experience I had with John Warren Cooke of Mathews County. Like Vernon Geddy, John Warren was a consummate Southern gentleman. When the *Richmond Times-Dispatch* hired me, the territory assigned to me included Gloucester and Mathews Counties. Dick Carter, the state editor, suggested that it would be polite to introduce myself to the man who published and edited local papers for each of those counties, to let him know I'd be operating in his backyard from time to time.

The publisher and editor of those weeklies was John Warren Cooke. I called upon him in his Gloucester office, but I did so with some trepidation. Not only would I be an intruder on his turf, I knew he was a man with immense prestige and political power, a veteran member of the Virginia General Assembly. But I needn't have worried. He welcomed and treated me warmly.

Not long after my first meeting with John Warren, he became Speaker of the House of Delegates, a position he held for a long time. Over the years when we met, he never failed to display the same courtesy and consideration he showed the first time.

In the 1970s, I was asked by my friends at the Virginia Department of Education to write and direct a film about the General Assembly that would be suitable for screening in junior and senior high schools. I suggested the possibility of using Speaker of the House John Warren Cooke, who probably knew more about the subject than anyone else, to tell the story, live and on camera. The department bought the idea and I was able to convince John Warren, who was in his final term in the House, that he could handle the task.

I scheduled some of the scenes in the old House of Delegates Chamber in the State Capitol, which had become a museum of Virginia history. One of its features was a life-sized statue of General Robert E. Lee in full uniform standing on the exact spot he stood when, in 1861, he accepted command of Virginia's military forces.

During a break in the filming, while the camera crew set up a shot, I sat with John Warren just a few feet from the Lee statue. Out of idle curiosity, not expecting an answer, I wondered aloud, "Did General Lee really look like that?"

John Warren didn't hesitate. "Exactly like him except that he wasn't in uniform. He wore civilian clothes."

I must have shown my astonishment, for he smiled at me. "My father told me." He turned toward the statue. "He brought me here for the dedication of that statue when I was a boy." Then he added, "My father served on General Lee's staff."

For a few unforgettable moments, I was in 1861, touching Virginia history.

The Farm

Probably none of the millions of people who visited Williamsburg during the years of the Cold War were ever aware of a local establishment that was probably better known worldwide than anything in the restored area. They didn't know that just a little more than a mile north of the city limits existed something called the Armed Forces Experimental Training Activity, a splendid example of government disinformation. The name was phony. Intelligence organizations everywhere in the world — and men and women who wrote spy stories — knew it as the Central Intelligence Agency's 'Farm', except that, until relatively recent years, not many knew exactly where it was. Novelists, for instance, placed it almost everywhere except near Williamsburg.

The CIA people in charge of the Farm maintained such a low profile and high level of security that Williamsburg residents seldom even thought about it, let alone wondered what went on behind its fences and armed guards. Except for a few local men and women employed there, there's little traffic through the main — and only — gate. That's because the CIA has an airport beside the York River, which is the main entry and exit to the Farm. Aircraft, including helicopters, provide a secure method of entry and exit, as well as a way to avoid the heavy traffic and tie-ups on I-95 and I-64 between Langley and Williamsburg.

Here's the Farm's genesis: During World War II, the farming community of Magruder, just outside Williamsburg, was confiscated by the government and its residents moved away. The area became Camp Peary, a training base for the Navy's Construction Battalions — the famed Seabees. Immediately after the war, the base was shut down and its buildings removed. The network of paved roads within the property was left in place.

In 1947, the Federal government gave the property to the Commonwealth of Virginia for ultimate development as a state park. That gift only lasted until 1949, when the Federal government took back the property and closed it to visitors.

Concurrent to those events, in 1947 Caroline was presented with a new Studebaker by her Auntie. With my help, she learned to drive on the road network inside the abandoned and state-owned Camp Peary. We enjoyed our trips around that former Seabee training base so much that after she learned to drive we frequently spent time there, for it was like having a huge park all to ourselves. We'd walk on the shores of the York River, investigate the foundations of wartime buildings, and picnic on grassy slopes while watching deer graze nearby. Thus it was a sad day when the former Seabee base was suddenly closed.

I suppose most Williamsburg folks were like Caroline and me. We wondered what was going on, but we didn't lose any sleep over it. Over the next few years, however, strange things came to my attention. First came an incident at my dentist's office over the Williamsburg Theater. Dr. Jennings Dorman was trying to save my teeth, so I visited him often. As I entered his office late one morning, three men brushed past me on the way out. When I sat in his chair, I needled him — something like, "Are you so hard up you have to take patients three at a time?"

Dorman didn't bite on my sally. He said, "I only treated the short one, but he couldn't speak English. The bald guy was his interpreter."

I tried to be funny. "Was it Greek to you?"

"I don't know what it was."

"So," I said, "why the third guy?"

Dorman shrugged. "I dunno, except I think he had a gun in a shoulder holster. I could see it when he bent over."

"Geez! I wonder where they came from."

My dentist frowned. "They didn't say, but you know, it's the first time I ever saw stainless steel teeth."

That was all, but it stuck with me. Then, within months, Thomas L. Thomas, a mailman in Williamsburg since 1928, provided more information. He delivered letters along Duke of Gloucester Street, including ours addressed to the Taliaferro-Cole Kitchen. Thomas was a friendly guy who almost always had time to chat, often beside the Pulaski Club bench while my oldest daughter played nearby.

"You know where I live?" he asked.

"On the road to Skimino?"

He nodded. "Yup, right across the road from the Camp Peary fence."

"I sometimes wonder what they're doing behind that fence," I said.

"I know one thing they're doing. They're dropping guys in parachutes into the base." Thomas shook his head. "A couple of days ago, one fellow's parachute hit some high-tension wires. Didn't seem to hurt him, though."

According to Thomas, most of the parachuting took place during daylight. "They jump in groups of four or five and I can hear instructions being shouted — 'keep your feet together, roll with it' — things like that." He said most of the chutists land inside Peary, but one night when one landed on his side of the fence, "I stayed up late to help him pick up his chute and drive him to the gate." I didn't think to ask Thomas if the chutist spoke English.

Today a pine forest screens the Farm's interior, but in the 1950s, the land was open — otherwise, the CIA wouldn't have dropped parachutists in the area.

More knowledge about Camp Peary came from one of my fellow volunteer firemen. He had a full-time Civil Service job as a fireman at Camp Peary. To his credit, he never violated the oath of secrecy he took before going to work there, but as one of our close-knit, boisterous organization of volunteers, he unwittingly gave us hints of what was going on behind the Peary fence. For instance, we realized he was fighting lots of fires with more and better equipment than was available to us in Williamsburg.

This tied in with what I learned from Pittman Roane, skipper of a buy boat named *Irene and Pearl* and operator of the York River Oyster Company. He complained that a couple of the men who supplied him with shellfish had been run away from waters where they'd been tonging

No welcome mat here! Close to Williamsburg is the entrance to Camp Peary, known around the world in espionage circles as the CIA's 'Farm'.

oysters for years. "Just off Magruder — you know, where Camp Peary is," Roane said. "I suppose the government didn't want them watchin' the planes landing and takin' off or the explosions and fires they could see from the river."

As a reporter, I was instructed by my managing editor — with whom I'd shared some of the knowledge I'd gained about Camp Peary — to see what information I could get legitimately by identifying myself as a reporter. So I called the phone number of the Armed Forces Experimental Training Activity and, after some delay, was connected to a man who identified himself as a captain.

After more delay, I was invited to call upon him about a week later. At the appointed time, I drove up to the gate. Two men in Army uniforms with MP armbands were on duty. Maybe they really were soldiers. With the CIA, one couldn't always be sure. They had me leave my car at the gate and a third soldier drove me to the administration building, where I was conducted to an office. A mature guy in the uniform of a Navy captain greeted me.

As instructed, I interviewed him about the activities being conducted by the Armed Forces Experimental Activity and he carefully answered all of my questions with sanitized double talk. (Journalists use an earthier term to describe it.)

I had requested a tour of the 'Activity' and sure enough, they gave me one.

I didn't let on that I knew the roads inside the gate better than they did. I knew what they didn't show me, which was almost as revealing as seeing it. So I thanked them profusely, returned to my office and called my managing editor. After he heard me out, he asked me to write a full report, describing what I had learned through both official and unofficial sources.

My newspaper, the *Richmond Times-Dispatch*, not willing to give aid and comfort to the enemy during the Cold War, never printed a word about the Farm. Instead, I've been told, our publisher showed my report to one of the senators from Virginia, who in turn showed it to Allen Dulles, head of the CIA. I suspect some tightening up of the Farm's security took place shortly thereafter, for my report revealed many of its secrets.

In December 1972 other news media announced to the world — and the Russians — the secrets of the Farm. Their revelations were not, of course, new to the *Times-Dispatch.* I'm proud to have been part of a newspaper which sat on that story for nearly twenty years, sacrificing the opportunity for a huge 'scoop' in order to avoid providing our Cold War enemies with any information about the Farm.

A Roller Coaster on Duke of Gloucester Street?

I met Peter Brown soon after he arrived in Williamsburg. He had been chief of the volunteer fire department in a small Colorado town, so it was natural for him to join our volunteers. In our organization, where the currency of friendship was neither social, financial nor occupational, Yale graduate Peter became one of the guys. We learned to enjoy and appreciate his acute sense of humor — particularly his unerring instinct for recognizing the phony or presumptuous.

Peter spent virtually his whole career with CW, ultimately earning a vice presidency. I think he would have been the perfect choice to become president. Unfortunately, he punctured pomposity and displayed common sense among stuffed shirts and dreamers. Such attributes made him unpopular among many of his Restoration peers, particularly those who seemed to float on a sea of self-satisfaction. Many were so busy pursuing their own agendas and protecting their turf that men like Peter Brown scared them witless — although there's reason to believe many were witless before Peter came along.

Peter Brown, CW vice president, Williamsburg volunteer fireman and one of the wittiest men in town.

From time to time over the years, a CW official would claim that the Restoration had to compete for visitors with Busch Gardens, the theme park built beside the Busch brewery six miles east of town. Like other wannabe Disney Worlds, it offers glitz, thrill rides and snake oil sales — all for a price, of course. The one near our town features 'The Old Country' — park areas called Germany, France, Italy and, for all I know, Lower Slobovia. I've heard you can spend as much in one of them in a day as you could if you actually went to Europe to see the real thing.

You may have inferred that I'm not a theme park fan. True. Having taken a grandchild to Busch Gardens in a weak moment, my attitude is based on experience. But I'm not anti-theme park. For folks who want to spend all that money on artificial thrills and phony experiences, that's their privilege. But like Peter Brown, I totally disagree with those Restoration people who believe they must compete for visitors with Busch Gardens — or any other amusement park, for that matter.

Peter and I amused ourselves one time figuring some of the gimmicks that CW might employ to compete with Busch Gardens. Right off, I suggested a huge roller coaster down Duke of Gloucester Street. Then Peter added a large water park on Palace Green and a two-level merry-go-round at the Powder Magazine — horses on the bottom, rocket ships above. We agreed the Palace and its grounds would be ideal for a wild animal park, with a railroad riding the visitors through it.

We believed restored Williamsburg should not compete with amusement parks with their shills and thrills. It is, or was intended to be, a historic monument, a reminder of the moment of greatness that spawned representative government, not only in America but throughout the world. It stands as a symbol of our great heritage, much like the Washington Monument or Lincoln Memorial.

The Street Where We (Used To) Live

On comfortable days in the spring and fall, I occasionally enjoy riding my bicycle on Duke of Gloucester Street. It's a nostalgic trip. I pass Nassau Street, where Caroline and I began our married life, and Bruton Parish Church, where we were married, and the site of the Travis House, where I worked my way through W&M.

Just as vivid — and not nearly as tough on my heartstrings — is a piece of street opposite the Powder Magazine. In the days when Duke of Gloucester Street was open to vehicular traffic, we routinely used it to respond to fire calls. During the day, if the town siren screamed for volunteer firemen, any of us close to the fire station on Henry Street raced there to man Engine One, the big Mack pumper. Arriving at a fire without firemen to fight the fire was prohibited, so the driver always waited for three or four us to arrive before leaving the station. We'd climb atop the hose load to don protective clothing — rubber boots, canvas jackets and hard hats stored in a rack beside the ladder.

If we turned down Duke of Gloucester Street toward the Capitol, we knew we were in for a thrill. As the pumper roared down the middle of the street with red lights flashing and siren blaring, traffic opened up before us. The driver, either Frank Epperson or Alvin Robertson, made sure the Mack reached take-off speed before reaching the old courthouse. That's because of the Parkway tunnel, which passes under Duke of Gloucester Street between the old courthouse and Chowning's Tavern.

The tunnel was built by digging a huge ditch across Duke of Gloucester Street, placing in it a round concrete vault like half of a huge drain pipe, then backfilling. Over the years, the fill had slowly settled on the sides of vault, leaving a large hump in the street. When Engine One hit the rise fast enough, those of us on the hose load became airborne. (If we didn't, the driver felt as if he'd failed in his job.) OSHA would never have approved, but we never felt that it was dangerous, and no one was ever hurt, probably because we always managed to have a hand firmly gripping the clothes rack, even with our legs high in the air while we convulsed with laughter.

That short piece of Duke of Gloucester Street was very familiar to me in other ways. As a W&M student I traversed it many times going to and coming from Chowning's Tavern. Later, when I clerked at the Lodge desk, Market Square Tavern was one of my responsibilities. And for many years, Caroline and I attended the annual lighting of a community Christmas tree across from the old courthouse. (Somehow that simple ceremony which attracted a couple of hundred local residents — and featured a brief talk by Mayor Polly Stryker before he lit the tree — grew into something known today as the 'Grand Illumination', which draws thousands of people each year.)

Duke of Gloucester Street around the tunnel hump was also the location I used on two different occasions to film Colonial Williamsburg's Fifes and Drums, known today as Williamsburg Field Musick. It's composed of teens who wear colorful red uniforms, march with precision and produce a marvelous 1776 sound.

The first occasion was during production of a motion picture for Vepco (now Dominion Virginia Power). A trucking shot was required, so in addition to arranging with CW for filming the Fifes & Drums, I had to obtain permission from the city — not CW — to use our camera vehicle on Duke of Gloucester Street.

That illustrates a point not fully understood by many folks: CW does not own the streets and sidewalks in the Historic Area. They are open to the public. Anyone can use cameras so long as they stand on public property and obey city laws. Williamsburg's city council controls traffic laws, including the right to close certain streets to traffic.

Some years after filming the Fifes & Drums for Vepco, I was commissioned by the Virginia Department of Eduction to direct an educational film. Its script called for a brief shot of the Fifes & Drums. There was no need to do a trucking shot. Since the Fifes & Drums routinely assembled at the Powder Magazine and marched across Duke of Gloucester Street to Market Square, I figured all we had to do was set up a camera on the grass between street and sidewalk and we'd get more than enough footage to meet our needs. We didn't need permission for this, but just to be polite, I called one of my friends in CW's public relations office (my recollection is that I spoke to Hugh DeSamper) to let the Restoration know what we planned and when and where we'd do it. He said there'd be no problem.

The morning came. We parked at the Lodge and the three-man crew carried the necessary camera and equipment down to Duke of Gloucester near the Powder Magazine and set up our shot.

"Get that damn camera out of here!" A heavy-set middle-aged man wearing a CW badge came charging up to us. "You can't film here without permission."

"We don't need permission to shoot here," I replied and then told the arrogant interloper to move off (not my exact words). Then I simply turned my back on him and reassured the cameraman and his helpers — all of them residents of Richmond — that everything was fine, just concentrate on obtaining good footage of the Fifes and Drums when they marched past us.

I knew that CW constantly received requests from advertising agencies seeking to use historic area buildings and/or backgrounds for TV commercials. This put the Restoration in a quandary. The folks in charge didn't want to give the impression that CW was commercializing its properties. As a result, they drew up an all-purpose reply to such requests which was a masterpiece. Although I can't recall exactly how CW worded it, the public relations office managed to imply that it was illegal to do any filming in the restored area without CW's permission. It did not tell the agencies that there was no law against filming from streets and sidewalks.

Incidentally, the CW man who tried to run us off didn't return. I was told that he was fired because he should have known people had

Except for local folks who drive on it to attend Bruton Parish Church, Duke of Gloucester Street traffic is normally limited to foot and bicycle traffic and occasional parades by Williamsburg Field Musick, better known as the Fifes and Drums, one of the most photographed subjects in restored Williamsburg.

the right to take pictures in the Historic Area from public property. I've always wondered if perhaps he had seen a copy of that letter CW sent to advertising agencies.

Four Roads to Jamestown

I'm a road freak — old roads, that is, including some that haven't been used for centuries. Today an ugly network of concrete or asphalt highways and streets attempt to carry an increasing volume of traffic in and around Williamsburg. Their straightening, widening and short-cutting have obliterated most of the roads which served the town for three centuries. Others have been blotted out by our runaway housing boom.

Fortunately there are still a handful of wonderful old roads in the area. In addition, traces of a few long-abandoned roads that used to connect Middle Plantation with Jamestown and other destinations can still be found.

The few surviving old roads that have never been "improved" by the heavy hands of highway engineers are not for high-speed travel or efficiency. They're crooked and narrow. They run between high embankments when going up or down slopes because of centuries of erosion. When they're not passing fertile farms, they tend to travel through tunnels formed by huge trees that often flank them. They're to be enjoyed for what they are: eye-filling reminders of our heritage.

There are a couple of such roads close at hand. One is Mill Neck, which winds uphill from Lake Matoaka to a connection with John Tyler Lane. Historically, it actually ran a slightly different course, veering off behind Number 207. Mill Neck is old, but I don't believe it's the oldest road from Middle Plantation to Jamestown. Another relatively untouched suburban route is Hickory Signpost Road, which connects John Tyler Highway with Ironbound Road. I've been told it follows an old Indian trail.

Green Springs Road, which links Route 5 with Jamestown, is also old, although I understand it doesn't exactly follow its original track. It has survived almost unscathed for nearly four centuries and from the ramparts of the reconstructed colonists' fort in Jamestown Settlement, it's possible to see a trace of where the 1600s Green Springs Road continued on to Glass House Point and Jamestown Island.

There are folks using Green Springs Road today who want it to undergo homogenization by the Virginia Department of Transportation, which would widen and straighten it. That would mean the loss of the trees that line it, a fate guaranteed to destroy its beauty and aura of history.

There are hauntingly beautiful old drives within a few miles of the historic area. One of the best is a short stretch of Jolly Pond Road which begins at James River Church on Centerville Road. About a mile or so from its beginning, it narrows to one-way traffic in order to cross the old dam which forms Jolly's Pond, then climbs between deeply eroded embankments to a small farming community identified to me years ago as Black Stump. For unadulterated scenic pleasure, that piece of county road is an Oscar winner.

Another favorite of mine is in the far northern part of James City County. To find it, take Croaker Road from Route 60, I-64 or

Jolly Pond Road as it crosses the dam which creates Jolly's pond. About a quarter of a mile beyond is an area of James City County known as Black Stump.

Rochambeau Road. Turn left at Garrett's Store (county Route 606). About a mile later, follow the paved road when it makes a hard left turn (Route 608). For about a half mile, you'll drive along a road that, except for an asphalt surface, obviously hasn't changed since colonial times.

Most of the old roads around Williamsburg — those that haven't been totally abandoned, that is — have been unalterably changed and lost to history, like the fate of Mooretown Road, which used to be the road to Richmond. And only a handful of elderly residents can recall grade crossings like Black's and Buell's on the east end of town, which allowed us to easily cross the C&O tracks from Pocahontas Trail to Merrimac Trail and vice versa.

Of all the old roads around Williamsburg, those that lead to Jamestown have fascinated me since the day I stumbled across an ancient causeway across College Creek about two or three hundred yards below the Lake Matoaka dam. Although it had obviously been appropriated by beavers, washed out and almost swallowed by the trees it supported, it was apparently man-made. Traces of ancient logs placed crosswise upon it indicated it may have been what's known as corduroy. But it's in a straight line above the level of the creek. Significantly, it's located far enough upstream to avoid being affected by rising and falling tides.

It was not high enough to serve as a dam (except for a beaver), so I believe it might have been used by Middle Plantation folks to cross College Creek on the way to Jamestown. The creek does not have a huge flow except in heavy downpours, so it could have served as a ford. I worked my way through the swampy thickets at each end and found traces of an old road leading away from it in both directions. On the Holly Hills side, it wound its way up to high ground and disappeared in what used to be farmland.

I tramped through the Holly Hill and Walsingham woods seeking traces of the road which led up from the causeway I'd discovered. I found two. One section was visible when the foliage was off the trees in a patch of woods left of the entrance to Walsingham (a new parking lot has destroyed most of it). The other, very visible, runs through the small city park opposite Walsingham at the intersection of Jamestown Road and John Tyler Lane.

It's my theory that these are traces of the first road between Middle Plantation and Jamestown, and that the second road to Jamestown is

Strolling on the trace of a road nearly four centuries old are Genevieve Stemann and her twin daughters, Audrey and Claire. Located in Geddy Park, opposite the Walsingham entrance, this was probably part of the original road from Jamestown Island to Middle Plantation. Modern Jamestown Road is in background.

what's now called Mill Neck Road. The two original roads intersected near the entrance to Professional Drive. From there a single road led to the Five Forks area, crossed Powhatan Creek at a ford, then connected somewhere beyond it with Green Springs Road.

Completion of the Colonial Parkway also ended the 15-year life of what I called "The Bridge to Nowhere" in a *Times-Dispatch* story. Construction of the Parkway, which began in the late 1930s, ended abruptly at the beginning of World War II. By then, the three-lane concrete road was completed between Yorktown and Williamsburg, including the tunnel under Duke of Gloucester Street. We could enter the Parkway from its terminus at Francis Street.

One other segment of the Parkway had been completed by the end of 1941, a three-lane concrete bridge across Halfway Creek. There it sat for 15 years, a bridge to nowhere. It was quite a sight, but to see it, one had to either obtain a boat and go up Halfway Creek from College Creek or struggle on foot through the overgrown construction road that led from South England Street. Parkway construction finally reached it in 1956. The long delay had obviously not hurt it, for today it's an integral part of the Parkway from Williamsburg to Jamestown.

Three other bridges constructed by the Park Service on that part of the Parkway have drastically affected boating on the James River in the Williamsburg area. One crosses College Creek at its mouth. Another bridges Powhatan Creek. The third is part of the artificial causeway connecting Jamestown Island and Glass House Point. All three provide a maximum clearance of only 12 feet at low tide for boats passing beneath them.

That 12-foot limit put Dudley Waltrip's marine contracting firm out of business. He had a small tugboat he moored at a dock he built on College Creek at the foot of the current airport. Although he did his best to fight the limitation, which prevented access to College Creek for his tug, the Park Service prevailed.

Waltrip had to give up his marine work, but not before he completed construction of the Jamestown Yacht Basin, which almost became a casualty of the 12-foot limit. As its name implies, it was probably designed to provide berths for sailboats. The bridge across Powhatan Creek killed that possibility, but it survived through the years because there's a shortage in this area of boat ramps and small boat piers available to the general public. Now there's a waiting list for slips at the Yacht Basin — but tall craft can't get in, short ones must retract their antennas, and flying bridges have occasionally come to grief on the Parkway pavement.

Chapter Eight

18th Century Meets 20th

To rebuild Williamsburg's historic area as it appeared in colonial times, some very clever — and expensive — modifications were made to provide modern services to folks who lived in restored homes. Telephone and power lines were buried, street lights disguised and fire hydrants camouflaged. And although exteriors of occupied homes conformed as closely to their 1776 appearance as painstaking research could make them, their innards were designed and built with up-to-date household conveniences.

Caroline and I began our married life in a carefully reconstructed colonial structure, the Taliaferro-Cole Kitchen on Nassau Street. It had all the modern conveniences, but two major flaws. For one thing, we had to keep our screen door locked in warm weather or discover tourists poking around the living room. For another, there was a lack of closet space. This was a universal complaint from housewives who lived in the historic area, but otherwise, living there was fun.

This was fine until the advent of television. Before the introduction of cable and other technological advances, Williamsburg's location in a TV fringe area meant that antennas were necessary to obtain decent pictures. Outside the historic area, all kinds of antennas sprouted on rooftops. But there's nothing in the history books that looked even remotely like a fringe-area TV aerial, so such devices were not allowed in the historic area. CW, which owned most of the occupied homes — generally rented by its employees — forbade them.

But residents, even loyal employees, wanted to see boxing, football, soap operas, *Dragnet* — even wrestling — on the magic boxes. And CW underestimated the residents' ingenuity. They found ways to beat the ban:

First, place an antenna in the attic. This worked unless the roof was lined with copper, which was the case with houses restored after World War II.

Second, look carefully at trees close to the house. Find a fork which faced in the right direction and had an appropriate angle. Attach rabbit ears inconspicuously and run a coaxial cable in through a window.

Third, use rabbit ears inside on the TV set. If nearby traffic wasn't too heavy and one didn't mind snow, fuzziness and occasional quintuple images, this was a fall-back solution.

Fourth and best, cultivate a close and abiding friendship with someone who lived outside the restored area with a 21-inch screen and rotating antenna.

Of course, the perfect solution came in 1973 when cable television arrived in Williamsburg.

Insanity Was No Excuse

During the 1800s and early 1900s, when the town languished in the doldrums, Virginians elsewhere in the state used the term 'going to Williamsburg' in a derogatory way. That's because of the presence of Eastern State Hospital, a mental institution. In the 1950s it was still there, ugly and shabby, at the edge of the historic area on the south side of Francis Street. Its main building replaced one that burned to the ground in 1885. The original structure had been as much a part of Williamsburg's colonial history as many of the better known exhibition buildings, for it was built in 1773.

In the 1950s Williamsburg's familiar scenes included an iron fence beside Francis Street along the Eastern State grounds. Except in bad weather, patients hung on the fence like concentration camp inmates to watch more fortunate people walk or drive by. Behind them, looming grimly amid the trees, was the ugliest collection of institutional buildings this side of the Gulag.

As a volunteer fireman, I had the opportunity — which I would gladly have passed up — of entering both men's and women's buildings when we were called for emergencies, often mattress fires. The conditions inside these three-story structures, which were like prison cages with locked doors and windows, is impossible to describe adequately. The smell of wooden floors — both men's and women's — impregnated with years of urine was enough to make us wish for our breathing apparatus. The sight of the patients locked up in those buildings — clothed, partially clothed or unclothed, with hair askew, no teeth and, in the case of men, unshaven — made me want to cry.

Although some local women's and church organizations did what they could to help the patients, they were overwhelmed. The problem, simply, was lack of funding. Dr. Granville Jones, the superintendent, couldn't find adequate help willing to work for the paltry wages the state paid and he didn't have nearly enough money in the hospital budget to upgrade or repair its buildings.

Most Williamsburg residents weren't really aware of Eastern State's dreadful shortcomings and the needs of its patients, but on hot nights in the summer, before the era of air conditioning closed our bedroom

---

Until the 1960s, the main entrance to Eastern State Hospital was on Francis Street between Henry and Nassau Streets, opposite what today is a parking lot. Mr. Rockefeller made possible moving the institution out of downtown.

The Library of Virginia

windows, those of us who lived in the historic area could hear the patients howling and screaming. Or, as Caroline put it one time, weren't they really calling for help?

Their savior was the same man who rescued Williamsburg from oblivion: John D. Rockefeller, Jr. In the mid-1960s his money funded moving the hospital into new buildings west of town. In return, the state turned the hospital's historic area over to Colonial Williamsburg. The ugly old prison-like buildings were torn down and the ground so completely leveled that — thankfully — no trace of them remains today. The original hospital building was reconstructed above ground. Beneath it, hidden underground, is the DeWitt Wallace Decorative Arts Museum.

Ha-Ha Was No Joke

Before it was rebuilt from the ground up, the Governor's Palace was nothing more than long-forgotten brick foundations near the C&O railroad tracks under the local high school. Working from old etchings and drawings, CW architects did their best to design a building — and its dependencies — that looks like the one that really existed in 1776. The result is impressive, and from the number of tourists who pay to visit it, the Palace is the most popular of all the restored buildings in Williamsburg.

What most visitors — and a lot of local residents — don't know is that there are some even longer-forgotten brick foundations not far from Five Forks which mark the site of a residence that was earlier, bigger and more elaborate than the Palace: Green Springs. Before the Park Service acquired the Green Springs property and closed it to visitors, Caroline and I visited the fascinating ruins several times. I've been told the old walls and foundations have been buried to protect them from further deterioration. The foundations were at the crest of a slope facing Jamestown. We could tell it was very wide because its ends were marked by curved walls.

At the foot of the slope were the remains of what at first glance seemed to be a sunken road or very large ditch. That, I was told, was the location of a ha-ha fence.

Ha-ha fence? Someone — I can't recall who — told us that a ditch was dug with a wall built on the side closest to the mansion, a wall invisible to occupants of Green Springs, but high enough to keep sheep or other animals from munching on the flowers which probably decorated the sloping ground in front of the building.

There Was Glory In It

For nearly thirty years, beginning in 1947, an outdoor drama staged in a 2,400-seat amphitheater on the shore of Lake Matoaka entertained visitors and residents on summer evenings. Written by Paul Green, Pulitzer Prize-winning playwright, *The Common Glory* combined music, dance

Walter Miller

The Common Glory, *performed in an amphitheater on the shore of Lake Matoaka, brightened and enlightened summer evenings in Williamsburg for nearly thirty years.*

and comedy with a stirring drama of the Revolution. Many local men and women, particularly those with William and Mary connections, participated in it, both on stage and behind the scenes.

In its early years, it offered colorful, tuneful and delightful performances that drew large crowds. But as the years passed, the show and its audiences withered. Williamsburg's weather was a handicap. The Matoaka Lake amphitheater, which faced the afternoon sun, soaked up its July and August rays. At curtain time, its wooden seats and asphalt aisles continued to radiate heat. On a 90-degree day with high humidity, that amphitheater was definitely not a comfortable place in which to sit. In addition, there were often late afternoon or early evening thunderstorms. Some summers they weren't frequent, but it wasn't necessary for a storm to strike. The threat of a storm kept people away.

There were other severe shortcomings, mostly traceable to the management — or lack thereof — provided by the state commission in charge of *The Common Glory*. Its chairman, a political appointee with the imagination of a concrete block, stayed in that position long enough to kill all vestiges of creative marketing, ticket sales, merchandising and staging. His invariable response to reduced ticket sales was to cut back the play's theatrical values. When it finally succumbed in 1976 to his inept management, *The Common Glory* was only a shadow of the drama which opened in 1947.

In spite of the problems hampering its final years, the summer production attracted performers who went on to fame and fortune elsewhere, among them Glenn Close, Goldie Hawn and Linda Lavin.

Fish Story

Not too many miles away from Williamsburg, on the Chickahominy River at the site of a colonial shipyard, is an abandoned building that once housed a unique seafood operation. Known as Menzel's, it was where watermen from throughout Tidewater sold their catches of catfish, turtles and eels. When I learned about Menzel's, I paid a visit and met one of the Menzels, who kindly showed me the operation and answered my questions, some of which were illustrations of my abject ignorance of the fishing industry.

I was astounded at the size of some of the catfish his employees were skinning and preparing for shipment to distributors. Twenty pounds was nothing. I saw some catfish that Menzel said weighed more than fifty pounds.

"From the James River?" I asked.

Menzel nodded. "And creeks and rivers from the Rappahannock to Currituck Sound. Most of them are caught on trot lines and trucked here."

I indicated a tank full of eels. "And them?"

He shrugged. "There are men who specialize in eels. They don't talk about how they get them."

"What do you do with them?"

"Ship 'em to Europe, air freight." Menzel grinned. "Not much market for eels in this country. Same with turtles."

Menzel's went out of business about the time of the Kepone scare, but I've been told that Kepone only affected fish from the James River, which was a small part of Menzel's business, that the real problem was the growth of catfish farms in Arkansas and other Southern states. Menzel's huge catfish required labor to prepare for marketing. Catfish from fish farms were all the same size when harvested and could therefore be packaged efficiently and economically.

Kidder Wasn't Kidding

E. Kidder Meade III was not a resident of Williamsburg long enough to become very well known and, as a further handicap, he worked in CW's highest echelon. But those were the only handicaps he couldn't overcome.

A chunky, freckled redhead from the Shenandoah Valley, Kidder was a West Point graduate who became a major in Patton's famous Third Army during World War II. While leading his battalion in Germany, he stepped on a land mine. It blew off both of his legs.

He came to Williamsburg as CW's public relations vice president about the time I became a reporter for the *Times-Dispatch*. Except for the rolling gait of a sailor at sea, I'd never have suspected he had any leg problems. In fact within moments of our introduction, in the hall outside his second-floor Goodwin Building office, I remarked that it looked as if he had a bad knee.

"I wish," he grinned infectiously, without explaining. Later one of his staff told me that Kidder walked on artificial legs.

Later, he offered to take me to lunch in his Jeep. As I slid into the seat beside him, he explained the vehicle's unusual controls. All of them had been altered so that Kidder could drive without using his feet — hands on, as he put it. I can't remember his ever again making any reference to his handicap.

For some reason, probably because I was always drawn to unpretentious, down-to-earth people, Kidder and I became friends. I often visited him in his Goodwin Building office. He seemed genuinely interested in anecdotes I told him about my experiences in the rural areas I covered. I was chagrined one day to discover that Kidder had accepted a position in New York with Earl Newsom and Company, at that time the country's outstanding public relations firm. That same day he let me have it with both barrels.

"You're always telling me how much you like your job," he said.

"Yeah, I think I'm pretty damn lucky."

"You believe that?" he frowned.

"Of course!"

Kidder shook his head in disappointment. "You're wrong, damn it." Before I could argue, he went on. "Everywhere you go, whether here in town or out in the counties, people are nice to you, aren't they?"

I had to agree. "Yup, I get along with them real well."

He shook his head again. "I bet you think they love you." He paused, then asked, "Are you that lovable?"

"What're you trying to tell me?"

"Do you have any idea what you really mean to the people out there? You represent the biggest, most powerful newspaper in Virginia. They're not going to do anything to upset you."

"It's not like that," I protested.

"You'll never know for sure, though."

I didn't know what to say.

"Look," Kidder became very sympathetic. "As far as I can tell, you're a pretty good reporter — just how good or talented I don't know, nor will you know as long as you're satisfied being a big fish in a little pond."

"But … what can I do?"

Kidder grinned. "Just hang on to your hat. When I get to New York, I might be in a position to steer you into something more challenging."

He was and he did.

The last time I saw Kidder was in New York City, the day he invited me to join him for a meal in the CBS executive dining room, where he served as public relations vice president for William Paley and Edgar Stanton. Fact is, that famous pair were at the next table as I tried my best to act as if I were accustomed to dining amid such folks.

I've often thought about that: Kidder Meade, a man with no legs, walking with giants.

Chapter Nine

My Williamsburg Hall of Fame

When I thumb through the pages of the *Virginia Gazette*, I'm impressed by the number of men, women and children who get their names mentioned or photographs printed. I'm also stupefied by the banality of many of them. I can't blame the *Gazette* for this. It's a given that the way to hold and/or increase circulation in a local publication is to print the names and photos of as many people as possible, people who want to be noticed by friends and neighbors — or acquire clippings to paste in a scrapbook or stick on the refrigerator door. So we encounter an overwhelming number of Little League baseball teams, garden club officers, guest speakers at Kiwanis, hospital volunteers — the list is almost endless.

It doesn't help that there are individuals who use participation in various causes as personal ego trips. They toss rocks in the water of public service, call the *Gazette* and swim in the ripples of recognition they create. Maybe they're trying to enhance their resumés or improve their reputations, but it's possible they're simply loading their obituaries with trivia.

There certainly are many men and women who serve the community who receive recognition for their contributions — and fully deserve the acclaim. But there also are some who perform service who are never noticed. The fact that many of them do not seek publicity makes it difficult to identify them. Nevertheless, I've run across a few who earned my sincere respect, not only for their contributions to others, but because they maintained a low — almost invisible — profile. Basically, I liked the way they lived, the way they worked and/or the good they did. None sought praise or recognition and might not even have been aware they'd done anything worth mentioning. I chose them for my own reasons.

I did not go through life seeking such people, but a handful left me with permanent impressions. There undoubtedly are others deserving of special recognition who escaped my notice, but here, in alphabetical order, are fifteen who unknowingly won membership in my personal Williamsburg Hall of Fame:

William J. Barnes

Bill Barnes, a member of William and Mary's Athletic Hall of Fame, came here as a freshman in 1978 on a basketball scholarship. He must have liked Williamsburg, because he never left town. After graduation, in between pickup basketball games with former teammates, he worked as an investment counselor. As time went on however, he discovered that basketball courts became longer, that he lost a step or two and that younger opponents were driving around him. But he persisted, for he loved the game too much to give it up.

Then, during the 1993–94 season Barnes was given an opportunity to coach the Walsingham Academy basketball team. This was by no

William J. Barnes

means an honor or a gift. It was not a paying job at that time. (Now he receives a token fee.) He would do his coaching when he could find time away from his full-time job. Worse, the prep school, though solid academically, had a small enrollment — male enrollment for the four high school years was only 120 — and was anything but a power in prep school basketball. In spite of such daunting difficulties, Bill took on the responsibility.

Not being much of a basketball fan, for a long time I knew him only as a conscientious, knowledgeable investment counselor, an ever-pleasant, helpful young man. He was such a nice guy I had the feeling he even tried to shrink in my presence to avoid towering over me. It was with some surprise that I discovered that Walsingham's basketball team has become a prep school power. Since the 1999–2000 season, it has reached the state prep school tournament every year, winning the prep school championship in 2001 and again in 2005. According to folks who know something about the game, credit for this remarkable turnaround belongs entirely to Bill Barnes, not only for his coaching ability but for the way he handles the teens who play for him.

Henry Billups

During my student days, William and Mary had 55-minute classes except on Saturday afternoons and Sundays. A bell in the Wren Building cupola rang on the hour to signal their beginning and rang again at five minutes before the next hour to mark their end.

That Wren Building bell was not automatic. A human being had to ring it. For years it was the task of Henry Billups, who kept track of the time on a large round watch — the kind railroad conductors used — that he kept in his vest pocket. Yes, he wore a vest. And a coat and tie too, for if ever a man showed dignity in his work, it was this tall, thin black man. He was so much part and parcel of William and Mary that he seemed to have been there forever. And in the eyes of youthful students, perhaps it was forever, for he went to work for the college in 1888 and was still on the payroll sixty years later.

The son of freed slaves, Billups couldn't remember exactly how old he was when he was hired to work in the college dining hall. He said he was "fo'teen or fi'teen" — but had no difficulty remembering he received six dollars a month plus his board. He also admitted that he made up in food what he did not receive in dollars and received tips from young men who sought special favors.

W&M Alumni Magazine

Henry Billups

Two years later, he was promoted to janitor and bell-ringer in the Wren Building — a tribute to Billups' dependability, for he was not yet twenty years of age.

For many years it was up to him to keep the entire building clean, its rooms stocked with firewood and their fires burning warmly. Even though the Wren Building was only two stories high until its restoration in the 1930s, Billups had a tough job until younger men were employed to relieve him of almost every job except carrying the college mail and ringing the bell.

Henry owned a home and lot on South Henry Street which were purchased by CW in order to build a fire station (since demolished and now location of the Seasons Arcade). Proceeds of the sale assured Billups of security for the remainder of his life. Sadly, almost all the men and women who knew him are gone. Soon he'll be part of the huge assemblage of Williamsburg characters who will only be recalled in books and memoirs.

Duncan Cocke

Newport News Daily Press

Duncan Cocke

Soon after local boy Duncan Cocke obtained his law degree, CW Executive Vice President Vernon Geddy chose him to be his legal assistant. Duncan delighted in recalling his first day on the job in April 1938: "There I sat, waiting to make important decisions, when [Geddy] walked in and presented me with the task of obtaining crow quills before that evening's harpsichord concert. The quills were needed for the jacks of the harpsichord. So I got up and went and shot a crow."

Counting summertime work in the 1930s, Duncan Cocke served CW for virtually fifty years, retiring as senior vice president. Carl Humelsine said of him,

"There are two people whose contributions to Colonial Williamsburg match Duncan Cocke's, and none who have served with such distinction for as long as he has. In every aspect of his work he has exemplified the highest standards of excellence."

The self-effacing Cocke summarized his career more modestly: "My job was to try to keep the organization from tripping over its own enthusiasm and getting tangled in its own complexity. It has been totally satisfying."

Duncan Cocke was a totally nice guy who compiled an outstanding record of service to Williamsburg and to William and Mary in a wide variety of capacities — and was duly recognized for his contributions. But that's not why he's in my Hall of Fame. I picked him because of the quiet, effective way he did his work for CW during half of a century — with loyalty, modesty and good humor.

Carl A. "Pappy" Fehr

Pappy Fehr became a member of the William and Mary music faculty in the fall of my junior year and immediately began planning to stage an elaborate choral celebration of Christmas. His idea was to combine the college choir, women's chorus and men's glee club in order to fill old Phi Beta Kappa Hall with the glorious sound of Christmas music.

There was only one catch. The college didn't have a men's glee club. Fact is, until the World War II veterans began to return to campus, there were hardly enough male students with vocal ability to fill a quartet. But this didn't faze Pappy. I think he went after every man on campus in an effort to find some who could sing.

He must have given up however, because he signed me as one of two second tenors. The other was Knox Ramsey (later an All-American football player). I think Pappy took us on simply to fill empty places in his planned procession, because neither of us could read music. At least Knox could sing after a fashion. Me? As the saying goes, I couldn't carry a tune in a bucket. During the performance, we simply went through the motions without making a sound, otherwise the real singers around us threatened dire punishment. That helped make Pappy's first Christmas extravaganza a huge success.

Subsequently, he organized and directed the choir which provided *The Common Glory* with outstanding music during its long summer seasons in the Lake Matoaka amphitheater. He also directed the choir of the Williamsburg Baptist Church. But Pappy was first and foremost a member of the William and Mary music faculty. In addition to his

W&M Alumni Magazine

Carl A. "Pappy" Fehr

teaching assignments, he was responsible for the college choir, which achieved an outstanding reputation during his tenure.

Former members of Pappy's college choir described his unusual but highly effective combination of discipline and humor. "We couldn't smoke," one man said, "and that was long before smoking became discredited."

A woman recalled, "We never read our music when we were performing. Pappy made us memorize every piece of music in our repertoire."

"He was a strict disciplinarian," another said, "but every once in a while, he'd relax and get us laughing. He had a marvelous sense of humor and knew when it was time to loosen us up."

Pappy, who was bald except for a fringe of hair around his ears, had a running gag. He took a large comb and cut away all of its teeth except for a few on each end. Then, during a rehearsal, when things became tense, he'd pull the comb from his pocket and go through the motions of combing his hair.

But, as another of his singers said, "Pappy's methods worked. I believe he could have created a choir from a collection of Barbie dolls."

John Green

After coming to Williamsburg from New York, John Green spent 26 years with CW, retiring as a vice president. He's the man who established and developed its visitor accommodations, restaurants and taverns — and ran them profitably and efficiently. He also acquired a

John Green

Courtesy of Joan Green Apter

small degree of fame because he commuted to his office at the Inn from his home on Jamestown Road by bicycle. He was far ahead of the rest of us in his belief in the importance of exercise. But neither his splendid achievements on the job nor his biking earned him a place in my Hall of Fame, however.

He's in my Hall of Fame because he is responsible for helping literally hundreds of William and Mary students earn college expenses through part-time jobs at the Travis House, Kings Arms Tavern and other operations under his management. Many years later he told me he had no choice about starting the program with sixteen young college men at the Travis House in 1944.

"It was wartime. I was ordered by [CW President Kenneth Chorley] to re-open the Travis House, which we had closed because of the lack of waiters. I had no idea where to find any, but Vernon Geddy [CW executive vice president] and Jack Pomfret [W&M president] came up with the idea of using college boys.

"I had real doubts about whether or not the arrangement would work, but those young men opened my eyes. Their enthusiasm, intelligence and eagerness to please our customers convinced me of their value."

After the war, of course, labor again became plentiful, but John Green saw to it that the arrangement with the college continued. In 1951, when CW replaced the Travis House with the much larger and more appropriate Kings Arms Tavern, more student waiters were employed. Thus, because of John Green's decision, the cooperative venture between the college and Restoration continued until 1992, when hotel employees formed a union. In the 48 years between 1944 and 1992, at least five hundred William and Mary students earned all or part of their college expenses at Travis House or Kings Arms Tavern.

J. Lesslie Hall, Jr.

Until the 1960s, Williamsburg fire protection and emergency medical service were in the hands of volunteer firemen. They knew that if they didn't respond when needed, there was no one else. So it was a point of pride — and motivation — for those men to respond to help their neighbors.

As the fire department became fully professional, the need for volunteers declined. They were relegated to backup status — available to help the paid men if necessary. But James City and York Counties began adding fire stations with professional firemen in the environs of Williamsburg. Today there are seven such stations, so professional backup help is always available. It seems there's no longer any valid need in Williamsburg for volunteer firemen.

But don't tell Lesslie Hall.

Known to many local firemen as 'Book', he's been a volunteer since second grade. That's when, at the age of eight, he raised forty dollars for the fire department by soliciting all the classes at Matthew Whaley School. In return, firemen always welcomed him at the fire station. During his frequent visits, he carried a notebook in which he recorded everything that happened. Thus the nickname, Book.

Lesslie returned to Williamsburg after earning a degree at Washington and Lee and joined the volunteers. He attended all the

J. Lesslie Hall, Jr.

necessary training courses to qualify as both a fireman and an emergency medical technician. He responds to fires and to rescue missions when necessary and has served as president of the volunteers so long most of us can't remember when he wasn't.

He continues the fund-raising activities he began at the age of eight and has led drives which over the years have provided the fire department with a variety of items not funded by the city, including a fully equipped ambulance, two utility pickup trucks and several sophisticated pieces of life-saving equipment. In 2005, he raised almost $40,000. Which goes to show that volunteers are still of value in Williamsburg and, most of all, the unpublicized leadership of Lesslie Hall.

James S. Kelly

I suppose I could have picked Jim Kelly for my Hall of Fame because he's the epitome of a nice guy. If anyone ever found something in Jim to dislike, I never met him. As far as I know, everyone likes Jim — and associates him with William and Mary, for he's a full-fledged college icon.

Jim got his degree in 1951, spent about a year in New York, which was all this native of Bristol, Virginia, needed before he hustled back to Williamsburg and took on the job of alumni secretary, a job he held until he moved up to the position of assistant to the president. This placed him in an office close to, in order, presidents Paschall, Graves, Verkuil and Sullivan.

Friends of mine who were aware I'd worked with Jim over the years used to ask me what kind of work he did for the presidents. Knowing his personality and his ability to soothe ruffled feathers wasn't enough to go on, so I wasn't able to enlighten them. I had my suspicions, however. It wasn't until the presidency of Tim Sullivan that I found out for sure what Jim did.

Another close friend, who served in the House of Delegates for many, many years, put it this way: "Jim Kelly was the oil that kept Tim Sullivan's wheels turning." In other words, he explained, Jim was William and Mary's best lobbyist. His work with legislators over the years, beginning for Davis Paschall, aided immeasurably in obtaining political and financial support for the college.

James S. Kelly

Jim's other behind-the-scenes contribution to his alma mater was probably even tougher. The typical scenario: A boy or girl is turned down by the admissions office for solid reasons. This often upset parents (or grandparents or close relatives). If they complain loudly to the president and they happen to be alumni or persons who might be important supporters of the college, the president usually turned the matter over to presidential assistant Kelly, hoping that Jim could soothe the disgruntled party.

I don't think anyone ever kept track of Jim's won-lost record in these cases, but on the basis of his personality and long tenure, I figure it must have been pretty good.

John Norwood

John first cut my hair in 1948. He still does. That's how long he's been a barber in Williamsburg. But as almost any of his customers can tell you, he's been much more than a barber. For one thing, they know he's been a news source in all the nearly 60 years he's been here. They also know that for many years, he was a regular participant in some of the best poker games in town. But there are a couple of things most folks don't know about him.

During the 1950s he was a volunteer fireman. This may not seem important, but when we had daytime fire calls, John's business location across the alley from the old Henry Street fire station made him immediately available at a time when most of the volunteers were at work in more remote locations. He left many a customer in the barber's chair in order to provide immediate manpower for firefighting. And among his volunteer peers, John's sense of humor was a huge morale builder.

But John had one secret very few of us were privileged to learn about. I learned it the hard way. When Caroline decided to remain at

John Norwood

home during the final months of her struggle with cancer, at times she seemed more concerned with the way she looked than with the disease. One day I mentioned this to John.

A couple of evenings later, he and his daughter showed up at our home with all their equipment and spent more than an hour fixing Caroline's hair. I hadn't asked for this, and when I offered to pay, John was insulted.

That's how I learned that for many years, John gave up his evenings in order to visit patients in hospitals, hospices or homes to provide haircuts for those who were in final illnesses or otherwise unable to travel. He has never asked anything in return or sought any recognition for it — and he does not know I'm writing this.

William O'Donovan

We've had a local newspaper in Williamsburg on and off for more than two centuries, *The Virginia Gazette.* When I arrived in town, it

William O'Donovan

was owned and operated by Alec Osborne and his sisters, Marian and Marguerite, and was for many years written, made up and printed in a structure behind the Goodwin Building that formerly housed Ayers Garage. The Osbornes did job printing too, probably as a means of keeping the *Gazette* alive, because I would guess that it wasn't all that profitable in those days.

The growth of Williamsburg was the beginning of the *Gazette's* rise from obscurity, but it didn't really blossom until William O'Donovan became its editor. Now he's the publisher.

In preparation for writing this book I decided to refresh my memory of local history. Plowing through microfilms of the *Richmond Times-Dispatch* or *Newport News Daily Press* — daily papers — would have been interminable, so I opted for the *Virginia Gazette*, a weekly which later became a bi-weekly. Until then, I confess that like Horatio Nelson, I may have been holding a telescope to my blind eye, for I hadn't paid much attention to the *Gazette*. That was a big mistake.

I discovered that the *Gazette* is an excellent record of Williamsburg's history since World War II. It's an even better record of the stewardship of Bill O'Donovan. His influence is apparent from the time he arrived, for he showed an unerring instinct for the town's core news. It isn't necessary to agree with all his editorials, but it's comforting to realize that he has his eyes and heart open. He not only shows affection for our community, he understands its problems.

James Patterson

Berkeley Pharmacy no longer exists, but while alive it was perhaps the most popular drugstore in town, probably because of its owner, Jim Patterson. He came to Williamsburg from Richmond in 1959 and opened a pharmacy in a small shopping center at the intersection of Jamestown Road and Route 199. When his business outgrew that location he moved to Williamsburg Crossing in 1988. His genial good humor — he almost always had a funny story ready to tell — and his business sense helped not only to develop a large clientele, but very loyal employees.

All that's great, of course, but by itself wouldn't put him in my Hall of Fame. It's what few people know about him that earned my respect. Here's a true story of one of his private, unpublicized acts:

Caroline and I lived in a wonderful waterfront home about fifteen miles from Williamsburg. In the fall of 1994, cancer-ridden, Caroline was in the final months of her life. She decided she wanted to spend her last weeks at home. Realizing her pain would become agonizing, Dr. Mark Ellis prescribed painkillers that I could administer in the absence

Courtesy of Robert Patterson

James Patterson

of an R.N. He told me to give Caroline a dose whenever she needed it, that all we could do was keep her comfortable.

I obtained the pain medicine from Jim Patterson at Berkeley Pharmacy. For two or three weeks, Caroline did not require many painkillers. With the long Veterans Day weekend approaching, I checked my supply on Wednesday morning, then, leaving a nurse to watch over my wife, I drove into town to obtain enough doses to carry Caroline through the upcoming holiday. As it turned out, Jim had just enough of the painkillers on hand to meet my need.

Thursday, without warning, Caroline's pain increased. I had to increase the dosage of painkiller. By Saturday morning, I realized that I might run out of painkillers before the pharmacy opened again on Tuesday.

I called Jim Patterson and asked for more of the medicine. Jim had none left in stock, but told me not to worry, he'd find more and get it to me.

In the meantime, a huge storm moved into the area, with rain sheeting down and gusty wind battering our waterfront home. Both power and telephone service went out and the nurse did not show up. I became frantic as Caroline's need for painkillers escalated and the supply diminished.

Then, well after ten o'clock that stormy Saturday night, there was a knock on the door. It was Jim Patterson, soaking wet, with a supply of painkillers. Unable to find any in Williamsburg or on the Peninsula, he had driven through the storm to Richmond, tracked down his distributor and made him go to a warehouse and obtain the necessary medicine!

People who worked for Jim Patterson told me that the incident was not unique, that Jim did things like that whenever the need arose.

Joyce Vaughan Robertson

During summer school terms in 1944 and 1945, one of the part-time jobs I held was lifeguard at the Williamsburg Inn swimming pool — the only outdoor pool in town. The Inn was closed for the duration of World War II, so CW opened the pool's membership to some of the town's leading families and recruited two or three college boys like me to be lifeguards.

Joyce Vaughan Robertson

With work schedules adjusted to fit classroom obligations, this was a plum job. Its only requirement was a Red Cross water safety certificate, which I had earned as a 12-year-old Boy Scout. It didn't pay much, but that wasn't the point. As a 22-year-old college student, I probably would have worked for nothing, because virtually all the young, attractive girls in town hung out at the Inn pool.

My enjoyment of those luscious teens sunbathing or floating past the lifeguard chair — particularly the one I ultimately married — was frequently interrupted by a scrawny, freckled pre-teen girl. This was 11-year-old Joyce Vaughan, one of Red Vaughan's bevy of daughters. She hadn't yet blossomed, but she had already acquired the ability to disrupt a young man's equilibrium.

If I dove from my elevated chair to escape Joyce's persistent attention, she'd dive right in on top of me. Until she came along I thought I was a pretty good swimmer, but she was a fish — more like a shark, actually. In an effort to evade her, I tried diving, executing my version of a jackknife or cannon ball. She followed so closely I feared for my safety. And when I attempted to escape by using the high board, Joyce not only followed, she passed me on the way down, laughing all the way.

I finally realized there was no way to beat her, so I joined her. For the better part of two summers, when I had free time we used the Inn pool as our playground, inventing outrageous double dives and risking our necks performing them from the high board. Joyce was fearless and I was afraid to let her know I wasn't.

Ultimately, the summers ended. Joyce and I went our separate ways. Not that we didn't hear about one another or run into one another from time to time — Williamsburg was a small town. I even heard she'd become active in women's softball, but didn't pay much attention, because the informant was my friend Dickie Gilliam, a former semi-pro baseball player noted for his wild stories and practical jokes. He enlivened a fire department meeting one night by telling the rest of the volunteers that a women's softball league was established in town by male softballers because they didn't want to have to compete with Joyce Vaughan.

That should have caught my attention, but when it came to softball, baseball or any sport played with a small sphere, I was totally uninterested, probably because I was nearsighted, had the reactions of a frozen turtle, and lost all my encounters with grounders. It took years for me to discover that Joyce Vaughan had earned regional, state and national recognition as a softball player.

The team she joined at the age of 12 dominated local women's softball for several years, largely because of Joyce's leadership and ability. Before long she was invited to play at a national level for a team known as the Bombers, based in the District of Columbia. She commuted there for practice sessions and competed with this team throughout America. The Bombers won national championships in San Antonio and Orlando. Twice Joyce won gold medals in the Senior Olympics.

After more than fifty years as a world-class softballer, Joyce retired. To fill her need for exercise, she took up golf. Male golfers should be warned that she shoots golf scores that match her age, which, truth be known, is in the 70s. Aside from her two Olympic gold medals, that alone merits a place in my Williamsburg Hall of Fame.

Pete Silver

I never spent much time in cemeteries until we buried Caroline in Cedar Grove. Then I became a regular visitor. After a few months, I discovered the city had employed a new caretaker. First thing I noticed about the man was his accent. It was pure Down East, as they describe it in New England. Natives of the Maine Coast speak it.

His name, he told me, was Silver. Pete Silver.

That brought back a long-forgotten memory. "I knew a guy in junior high school in Massachusetts whose name was Silva. He said he descended from Portuguese fishermen who used to fish in the Grand Banks, then settled in Maine," I said. "He told me he had some relatives who changed Silva to Silver."

Silver grinned. "You got it. He might have been a cousin."

I began paying more attention to Silver. The previous caretaker had not done a very good job. For one thing, he hadn't enforced the city's rules about decorating gravestones. The result was a hodgepodge of garden plots around some stones and weeds obscuring others. Pete

Pete Silver

patiently worked with families to make them familiar with the rules and slowly cleaned up the grounds.

With clutter removed, Pete was able to do a much more effective job of mowing and trimming around and between the graves. But that was just the beginning of his service to those who came to Cedar Grove. He was patient, understanding and sympathetic with everyone, the bereaved who arrived to arrange for burials or those who were seeking genealogical information. He just did an incredible job.

Knowing he was from Maine, I mentioned to him that I'd seen a television documentary on a murder case in Portland. Pete nodded. "Yeah. I worked that case."

I immediately jumped all over him. What did he mean by saying 'he worked that case'?

Then it came out. Pete had retired as a lieutenant in the Maine State Police. Then he invested his savings in a convenience store in a good location. When his wife developed a crippling disease, she decided she'd like to move to the Williamsburg area, where their daughter lived and which had a much milder climate. So Pete hurriedly sold his business. In the process he made a big mistake. For the sake of a quick sale, he financed the purchase himself. When the buyer went broke, so did Pete.

Since his retirement pay was not sufficient to live on and support his wife's medical needs, Pete had to go to work again. He was over-qualified for the work he was performing, but I never heard him complain. He just went ahead and did his best.

Bob Vermillion

Almost immediately after we organized a rescue squad in the fall of 1950, Williamsburg's volunteer firemen encountered a basic problem: there was no emergency room in Williamsburg. Dr. Bell's tiny private hospital could not deal with seriously injured accident victims. Depending upon which was closest, we rushed our patients either to Riverside Hospital in downtown Newport News or to Medical College of Virginia Hospital in Richmond. This meant that for long periods of time our ambulance was not available for other emergencies.

When Bob Vermillion, owner of Watts Motor Company on York Street, learned of our problem, he began providing us with two Chevrolet station wagons every year. They weren't as roomy as regular ambulances, but they made it possible to handle more than one call at a time. A couple of years later he donated a new truck, which made possible our acquiring a multi-purpose emergency vehicle. We recognized Bob's generosity by making him an honorary member of the fire department. This was not an honor we bestowed upon many people.

Thomas L. Williams

Robert Vermillion

Bob Wallace

Bob Wallace was often blustery and loud, but very few realized — as I did — that he was actually one of the most self-effacing men in town. He operated a couple of businesses, including the College Shop on Duke of Gloucester Street, but was probably best known for his Christmas tree. Bob and his wife had a lovely home on a bluff above the Lake Matoaka dam, which was visible to anyone driving down Jamestown Road from town (the house is still there). On the lawn in front was a large, well-shaped tree. Decorated with white lights, it was a wonderful sight during the holiday season.

Like the tip of an iceberg, the house and tree didn't tell anything much about the real Bob Wallace. Many local folks, women in particular, were turned off by his physical appearance and gruff, coarse manners. Writing that he looked like an unmade bed might be too extreme, but Bob indeed was large and not particularly concerned with his attire. And he did utter crude remarks at inopportune moments, but that was all on the surface. Below that dwelt a very good and able man.

One area of Bob's life which only a handful of people ever learned about was his generosity. He apparently never said a word to anyone about this, but from other sources I learned long ago that Bob made it possible for many young men to obtain college educations. No one will ever know for certain how many he helped with direct financial assistance, but there may have been as many as ten. Most of them were local youths whose families could not afford to send them to college.

Robert Wallace

Courtesy of the Wallace Family

His greatest civic contribution to the Williamsburg–James City area came as a result of his long service on the school board. Both City Manager Hugh Rice and Superintendent of Schools Rawls Byrd told me — independently — that had it not been for the contributions and influence of Bob Wallace over the years, the school systems of Williamsburg and James City County would have remained independent of one another. The savings effected by their consolidation would have been lost.

Billy Woodbridge

Back in the days before e-mail, messaging cell phones and all the other kinds of electronic wizardry drowned us with communications, messages to out-of-town individuals or businesses were conveyed either by telephone or by telegraph. That made the local Western Union office — on Richmond Road adjacent to the Kappa Kappa Gamma house — an important address in Williamsburg, and Billy Woodbridge one of the best-known and most recognizable young men in town.

I have no idea how many years he was our Western Union messenger, but I will always visualize Billy as a teenager in his dark green uniform and cap, with clips at his ankles to hold his trousers in place, earnestly peddling his beat-up bicycle around town no matter the weather, his face fixed with determination as he sped to deliver the telegrams.

Billy deserves a place in my Hall of Fame, not only because of his dedication to doing his job properly, but for something else. Invariably cheerful, he spoke in staccato bursts. That's the only outward indication I ever detected that showed Billy was what today's experts would describe as 'mentally challenged'.

I think Billy Woodbridge met that challenge and won hands down.

With the demise of telegrams as tools of communication, Billy worked at a number of places. His last job was as dispatcher for a taxicab company, where he met a tragic end: beaten to death with a hammer by drug addicts seeking the company's petty-cash box.

Courtesy of Winni Baker

Billy Woodbridge

Chapter Ten

The Town That Disappeared

Over the years I've attended many burials in Cedar Grove Cemetery — too many, as I think about it — so I can't recall whose had occurred the day I walked down the drive with Bill Person (Judge Person's father). We were on our way to where we'd parked our cars when suddenly he stopped, brows furrowed.

I feared he was having a seizure. "Are you all right?"

Bill shook his head.

"What's wrong?" I asked.

He turned to look back at the array of tombstones behind us. "I just realized I know more people in here than I know in town."

Perhaps I wasn't old enough or maybe the town hadn't yet outgrown my circle of friends and acquaintances, because at that moment I didn't comprehend the significance of what he said. Now I do. These days when I visit Caroline's grave I often take time to walk or drive among the other tombstones. It's amazing how many of the names are familiar. They weren't all necessarily close friends, but I know who they were — men and women among whom I lived during most of a lifetime. They're part of the Williamsburg that used to be.

It's not only the names on Cedar Grove tombstones that speak to me of that old hometown. I get the same sort of feeling when I visit the business block of Duke of Gloucester Street (I'll never get used to calling it Merchants Square). I don't go there very often, because it offers nothing for me except memories. I never see anyone I know. Except for a couple of new structures, the buildings haven't changed, but virtually every establishment and office is different from those I knew when this was downtown Williamsburg. They're like the gravestones at Cedar Grove. They mark a town that died.

CW has installed benches in shady areas of the sidewalk. I like that. We didn't have anything like them when the business block was the center of town. But then we didn't have to rest tired old legs, and of course we didn't have any reason to sit and remember how it was. We were busy living in it.

Now I can sit in front of the Williamsburg — oops, Kimball — Theater and allow memory to take control of my imagination. Across the street, the Trellis becomes Rexall's Drugstore, and inside, I visualize the soda fountain where we met to match chits for coffee. Next door, there's a window display in the Christmas Shop that becomes the entrance of the post office arcade. And just to the left, Pender's Grocery overpowers today's Toymaker.

In my reverie, the street isn't empty. Right off I can see big Bob Hornsby and his gorgeous wife, Lois, in front of Frazier-Graves Men's Store. There's a youngster with them, probably their son, Bruce. Nearby, Walt Miller stands in the door of his camera shop. Beside it there's a familiar entrance to stairs leading to the second floor. It pains me to realize that now someone is selling expensive lingerie up there where the *Times-Dispatch* bureau and accountant Fred Flanary had offices.

In the alley leading to the parking area behind Miller's, our Red Cross lady, Marian Chess, is chatting with Charlie Hackett and Tommy Savage. According to Caroline and several of her lady friends, they're two of Williamsburg's most attractive men. They're also — among men — the most popular. Charlie, a stalwart member of the volunteer fire department, served several terms on city council. Tommy wasn't so lucky, struck down in the prime of life by a crippling disease.

Those fragments of memory are so strong I try to change my mood by leaving the comfort of the bench to walk toward Henry Street. A few paces past the theater, I'm reminded of Schmidt's Florist and visualize Mrs. Schmidt and Blair Burleson checking the window display. Close by is the state ABC store, our only source of legal liquor, which doesn't open until 10 a.m.

As I pass the Five and Ten and the A&N Store next to it, I wave a greeting to Smitty, the A&N manager (no one knew his first name was Charles), who wore a pencil-line mustache at a time when facial hair was not popular. He's out front laughing with attorney A.B. Smith and John Dye. Two of John's taxis are parked nearby. When I reach the corner of South Henry Street, in front of the A&P, I look across Duke of Gloucester Street at Casey's Department Store, like the Peninsula Bank an anchor of the business block — but there were folks who said the real anchors of the block were its Greek restaurants. At one time there were three, but later there were just two.

Then for some reason I look back up the street toward the ABC Store. I see the sidewalk around it as it looked on a typical Saturday morning — seething with a happy, laughing crowd of black men and women. I knew many of them and I knew why they were there. Many might buy a pint or two of liquor at the state store, but that was not the main reason they gathered there. Most worked at hourly jobs for five days. This was their once-a-week opportunity to meet friends to exchange gossip and swap stories. Members of the white community did the same thing over coffee on a daily basis in Rexall's.

Then, as happens so often, my thoughts return to the present. I ask myself the same haunting question: What became of the old business block?

As a reporter, I should have been more aware of what happened, but all I can recall is that at some time during the 1950s, Colonial Williamsburg decided to build a shopping center at the corner of Richmond Road and Monticello Avenue (which didn't exist then). Construction on the 22-acre site began in 1955.

Like many other local folks, I wondered about the need for a shopping center in Williamsburg, particularly at a location so far out of town — it was a mile from Duke of Gloucester Street. And why would CW, landlord of all the business block, want to compete with itself? Like almost everyone else, I shrugged it off as none of my concern and went on with my own business.

Shortly thereafter I left the *Times-Dispatch* and moved to Richmond to pursue a new career, but as Caroline put it, we never really left Williamsburg, for we continued most or our associations and never missed a holiday reunion with her family. Nevertheless, it wasn't until we moved back to Williamsburg that I became fully aware of the huge changes that had occurred in the business block. No records remain to reveal how many merchants lost their business block leases and were forced to move out. When enough of them had left, others followed because the number of local shoppers declined, replaced by growing numbers of visitors who weren't interested in buying groceries or hardware. Many of the former business block operations relocated in CW's shopping center, but a few went out of business, and some found other locations. Rose's Five & Ten and Madison's Gifts hung on until CW cancelled their leases in 1982. The published explanation: CW said it wanted to make 'Merchants Square', as they named it, the most distinguished shopping place in the country.

Here's a list of some of the businesses which disappeared (since I relied upon my memory, it may contain inaccuracies and omissions): ABC Store, A&N Store, A&P, Albert Douglas' bakery, College Pharmacy, Colonial Restaurant, Frazier-Graves Men's Store, Howard Johnson Restaurant, Pender's, Peninsula Hardware, Miller's Camera Shop, and Schmidt's Florist.

With the closing of Casey's Department Store a few years before this writing, only the Peninsula Bank (now Sun Trust) and College Shop now remain of all the businesses that flourished in the first block fifty years ago. Not that there aren't stores and restaurants in the business block, renamed Merchants Square. There are — and they're pretty much the kind you'd expect to see on Fifth Avenue, on Rodeo Drive or in West Palm Beach.

There's one operation in Merchants Square that remains to attract local residents. It's the old Williamsburg Theater, refurbished and reborn as the Kimball Theatre. However, where it used to offer popular movies, its current programs are designed to attract folks with upscale tastes in art and entertainment. That means the well-educated, financially comfortable retirees (or wannabe's) who make up a large part of the Williamsburg area population, probably the same kind of people who recognize the names of the stores that now occupy Merchants Square.

I understand that most of these establishments are operating profitably, which means that CW is — or should be — collecting substantial rentals. So CW's real estate business is successful. It's making money — but I can't help but wonder if that's why Mr. Rockefeller gave his millions.

Conclusion

Twice in the past 30 years I've written and assembled slidefilms about the town I adopted as my own. The first, honoring the 50th anniversary of the Restoration in 1977, was narrated by Bud Geddy at a dinner at the Lodge. The second, designed to resurrect 1950s Williamsburg, was presented at the 1994 dinner meeting of the Williamsburg Reunion, a biannual gathering of old-time residents.

I had no purpose in creating either of those slidefilms other than to press the nostalgia button, to express my devotion to the Williamsburg of earlier days. Neither program covered all the material available. Recently, after taking another look at the two scripts, I realized I hadn't done all I could have done. I assembled unused notes, articles, anecdotes and photos with the idea of writing this book to show how my affection for Williamsburg developed and to pay tribute to the men and women who shared the town with me. As I organized the material, researched the subject and began trying to give it some kind of shape, I realized how much I miss it. I loved that Williamsburg and its people. Writing about it gave me both joy and heartache, often simultaneously.

I can't say that I love today's Williamsburg, but even if it doesn't generate the same kind of affection I hold for the town that was, it remains a fine place in which to live — and I don't want to live anywhere else.

Williamsburg has attracted thousands of new residents. Many are good neighbors, but I often get the feeling that they didn't come here to be Williamsburg people, that they've brought their suburbs here along with their baggage, furniture and golf clubs.

I run into a problem when dealing with them. If I refer to men or women of my old Williamsburg, I have to provide them with biographical backgrounds, and if I happen to mention a place or road we knew in Williamsburg's salad days, I have to draw a map for them. So I much prefer being with the handful of men and women who share the same memories of the wonderful Williamsburg that no longer exists. We're a dying breed, of course. But perhaps when we're all gone, this book will bring them and our town briefly back to life. It's a shame folks will only know my old hometown by reading about it.

That doesn't even come close to having lived it.